Contents

English for Primary Teachers

A handbook of activities and classroom language

MARY SLATTERY

JANE WILLIS

OXFORD
UNIVERSITY PRESS

OXFORD
UNIVERSITY PRESS

Great Clarendon Street, Oxford OX2 6DP

Oxford University Press is a department of the University of Oxford.
It furthers the University's objective of excellence in research, scholarship,
and education by publishing worldwide in

Oxford New York

Auckland Cape Town Dar es Salaam Hong Kong Karachi
Kuala Lumpur Madrid Melbourne Mexico City Nairobi
New Delhi Shanghai Taipei Toronto

With offices in

Argentina Austria Brazil Chile Czech Republic France Greece
Guatemala Hungary Italy Japan Poland Portugal Singapore
South Korea Switzerland Thailand Turkey Ukraine Vietnam

OXFORD and OXFORD ENGLISH are registered trade marks of
Oxford University Press in the UK and in certain other countries

ISBN-13: 978 0 19 437563 4

Only available as pack with CD:
ISBN-13: 978 0 19 437562 7

Typeset by G.M Brasnett, Cambridge
in Thesis TheSans and TheSerif

Printed in China

ACKNOWLEDGEMENT
Designed by Peter Burgess

Acknowledgements

We would like to thank most sincerely the many people who have in one way or another contributed to this book.

Our special thanks must first and foremost go to all the teachers world-wide who recorded their classes for us and sent us their recordings to help us design and write the units. Their co-operation meant that we had real language from real lessons to put in the book. (See page 143 for information about the teachers.)

We are equally grateful to the children in the following classes and schools for allowing extracts from their lessons to be used in the units.

First Grade and Third Grade of El Colegio de Infantil y Primaria Antonio de Valle Menéndez de Garachico, Tenerife, Canary Islands.

First and Second Grades of the YMCA English Language School in Sagamiono, Japan.

First, Third, Fourth, and Fifth Grades of the SEV Primary School, Göztepe, Izmir, Turkey.

Second Grade of Colegio Público Arquitecto Gaudi, Madrid, Spain.

Third and Fourth Grades of Meiji Gakuen Primary School, Kitakyushu, Japan.

Third and Fourth Grades of the Scuola Elementare 'G. Giusti', Istituto Comprensivo Massarosa 2°, Lucca, Italy.

Third Grade of the Scuola Elementare 'G. Cena' di Cisterna di Latina, Italy.

Fourth Grade of Colegio Público, Beata Agnes, Beniganim, Valencia, Spain.

Sixth Grade of Colegio Público, Aguañac, El Tablero, Gran Canaria, Canary Islands.
The REJ English House in Ena-shi, Gifu-ken, Japan.
Second and Fourth Grades of Primary of the CEP Julio Pinto at Tres Cantos, Madrid, Spain.

We would also like to thank
— the many teachers we have worked with over the years on training courses and in workshops who knowingly or unknowingly contributed ideas for this book, and especially Linda Aytan and Elisabeth Orbaşli for their comments and suggestions at the later stages.

— the teachers and trainers who read and commented in detail on the units as they were written and who suggested many improvements. Their enthusiasm and helpful feedback made our task easier and more enjoyable. They were: Éva Benkö (Hungary), Kim Bradford-Watts (Japan), David Carless (Hong Kong), Chang Shiang-Jinn (Taiwan), Jennifer Jarvis (Great Britain), Lo Chun-Tien (Taiwan), Saro Manrique de Lara (Spain), Adriana Mizukami (Brazil), Silvana Rampone (Italy).
— Hazel Geatches for videoing many of the lessons.
— the talented actors – adults and children – who re-recorded extracts from the material sent in by teachers and their classes.
— the staff of The Sound House Ltd recording studios and most particularly Peter Marsh (Sound Editor) of OUP for their expert and meticulous work in putting the CD together.
— the designers, typesetters, and illustrator for their invaluable contributions to the book: Peter Burgess, Mark Tilley-Watts, Graham Brasnett, and Jeff Borer. Illustrations by Ann Johns. Cover design by Jo Usherwood.

I, Mary, would like to thank my colleagues at the Applied Language Centre in University College Dublin, especially Mary Ruane (Director), Ciara Madden, Michael Flannery, and Rachel McDonnell, and colleagues elsewhere, in particular Margarita Mele, for their continuing support and encouragement.

I, Jane, would like to thank my colleagues at the Language Studies Unit at Aston University, Birmingham, England for their support and those teachers participating in the Aston Masters in TESOL Programme who offered ideas and sent in additional recordings. I am also very grateful to Margaret Allan and Dave Willis for their suggestions for the Introduction.

We would both like to thank our families and close friends for their understanding and support during the months we were busy writing this book.

And finally, a very big thank you to our editor Julia Sallabank – not just for her detailed feedback and careful reading of the manuscript but also for her generous and positive support at every stage of the book's development.

Symbols used in this book

The authors and publisher are grateful to those who have given permission to reproduce the following extracts and adaptations of copyright material:

page 28 'Physical break chant' by Ronald Woods and Bill Bowler. From *JET Magazine* October 1990. Copyright Mary Glasgow Magazines/Scholastic. Reproduced by permission of Mary Glasgow Magazines/Scholastic.

page 37 'Monster game' by John Clarke and Julie Ashworth. From *JET Magazine*. Copyright Mary Glasgow Magazines/Scholastic. Reproduced by permission of Mary Glasgow Magazines/Scholastic.

page 45 'Chanting is fun' by Carolyn Graham. From *JET Magazine* May 1993. Copyright Mary Glasgow Magazines/Scholastic. Reproduced by permission of Mary Glasgow Magazines/Scholastic.

page 87 'A party at Croco Bay'. From *Operare nel Modulo, 2º ciclo* by Alessandra Brunetti, Theorema. Reproduced by permission of Petrini Editore.

page 101 Extracts from *Elmer* by David McKee (ISBN: 0 86264 208 6). Reproduced by permission of Andersen Press Limited.

page 110 'Mr Caterpillar's strange adventure' by Claudia Baruzzi. From *JET Magazine* Vol. 3, Issue 9. Copyright Mary Glasgow Magazines/Scholastic. Reproduced by permission of Mary Glasgow Magazines/Scholastic.

page 145 (Glossary): We are grateful to Oxford University Press for permission to reproduce and adapt definitions from the *Oxford Wordpower Dictionary*.

We are also grateful to Oxford University Press and Pura María García for permission to reproduce extracts from the *Fanfare* teacher training video in the book and CD.

Words in **bold** are used in a specialist sense, and are explained in the Glossary (pages 145–6).

🎧 listen to the CD or your cassette copy.

➲ here you need to DO something, not just read. Take time to think about it and follow the instructions carefully. If possible, discuss this with someone you know.

RECORD record yourself doing this, for effective learning and fluency practice.

o⊸ this means that this question/exercise/ activity has sample answers in the Key (pages 135–9).

About the Authors

MARY SLATTERY is a teacher and freelance teacher trainer. She began her career in the 1970s teaching English and Spanish in Dublin, Ireland. In the 1980s she started to teach English as a foreign language. She has taught children and adults at all levels and has written articles on various aspects of teaching.

For the past 12 years she has designed and worked on short English language training courses for non-mother tongue primary teachers at the Applied Language Centre in University College Dublin and has given workshops in Europe. She works on Certificate and Diploma teacher development programmes and on short courses for international groups of teachers of English.

Mary is particularly interested in second language learning through storytelling and arts activities. One of the main influences on her teaching was her mother who taught her through Irish and English. She is married and has three sons.

JANE WILLIS began her career teaching French and English in Africa, and for the next 20 years she taught English and trained teachers in many different overseas countries. On returning to Britain she worked as a writer and freelance teacher trainer and consultant, often going overseas to run workshops for non-native speaker teachers.

She has written many articles on ELT and several books for teachers, two of which have won prizes: *Teaching English Through English* (Longman) and *A Framework for Task-based Learning* (Longman).

In 1991 she joined the Language Studies Unit of Aston University, Birmingham, England, where she works with practising teachers of English at all levels, world-wide, on Distance Learning programmes leading to a Masters in TESOL/TESP.

Jane is married (to another English teacher!) and they have two daughters and several grandchildren. Her pastimes include walking in the mountains, sailing, and being entertained by her grandchildren.

Introduction

As English is being introduced into primary classrooms round the world, more and more teachers are being asked to teach English to Young Learners. This book was written to help such teachers to improve their spoken English and to use it effectively to help their children learn.

This book is for teachers who teach English to children aged 4–12, including:

— **generalist teachers:** i.e. class teachers, who teach all subjects as well as English to one class
— **specialist language teachers** who teach English to several different classes and levels
— **teachers on training courses** (there are lots of practical ideas to try out)
— **tutors on a training course** for primary teachers of English (in-service or pre-service)
— **teachers who want to study at home** (the units are carefully graded).

The book will help you

— to improve your confidence in speaking English in the classroom
— to broaden your range of language teaching activities.

The activities and language will be relevant to your classroom because

— the syllabus for the book comes mainly from our 'bank' of English lessons recorded and contributed by thirteen different teachers from countries round the world. These lessons are samples of good practice from dedicated and committed teachers – not perfect samples specially prepared, but real classes in action.
— they include a wide range of activities and techniques used by teachers and trainers from different parts of the world and include popular activity types from primary textbooks
— we have selected classroom extracts and examples of language that are typically used by successful non-native primary teachers internationally. Our aim is to provide coverage of classroom English in normal everyday settings – not in idealistic situations.

— the classroom language is carefully graded. Unit 1 begins with basic classroom instructions for a typical lesson. The next units cover specific language relevant to particular activity types. In the final units we shift the main focus to longer stretches of talk, for example, telling a story.

If you work through the book and CD you will

1 find many practical ideas to adapt and try out in your lessons
2 activate the English that you already know and gain the confidence to use more English with your pupils
3 benefit from other teachers' experience by hearing typical samples from everyday English lessons. These are real lessons taught by primary teachers (both non-native and native speakers) around the world, but they have been re-recorded in a studio for this book
4 expand your range of classroom language. This will help you to:
    — carry out day-to-day classroom organization in English
    — manage each basic activity type in English
    — give your children a rich experience of English of different kinds – from short, simple instructions (for example, Total Physical Response and questions and answers) to longer, **sustained** talk (for example, storytelling)
    — talk to your learners about topics which interest them, and themes that young learners' coursebooks and syllabuses generally cover
    — know when it is helpful to use the children's mother tongue, and when to allow children to use their mother tongue.
5 be well prepared for future professional development.

To summarize, we recognize that teaching English can be more rewarding and less stressful if you
— feel confident enough to use English as the main language in the classroom during English lessons – giving your young learners valuable experience of English in use

— have a wide variety of activities that are both fun for young learners and rich in natural language learning opportunities.

This book aims to demonstrate effective language teaching in practice; it rests on sound educational principles and up-to-date theories of child second language acquisition. However, it does not attempt to explain issues in general primary pedagogy or educational psychology.

Working your way through the book

The first unit asks you to reflect on the processes of language learning and to examine ways to create effective learning conditions in class. It also introduces you to the study methods used in the book.

Units 2 to 5 cover listening then speaking activities. Units 6 and 7 deal with reading then writing activities. The next two units illustrate ways of using stories. The final unit covers wider issues such as use of mother tongue, correction, integrating coursebook activities, and lesson planning.

We look initially at the four skills of listening, speaking, reading, and writing separately. We do not recommend they are treated separately in class, but we want to focus on the different challenges that each skill presents to you, as teacher, and to your learners.

Activities for listening and speaking early in the book are recycled and extended in later units. Nearly all the activities recommended are ones actually used by the teachers who contributed their lessons to this book.

How the CD can help you speak English in the classroom

The CD contains 62 recorded extracts from typical English lessons as well as some pronunciation exercises. It forms an integral and vital part of this handbook.

Listening to the lesson extracts gives you first-hand experience of teachers in action. They include typical classroom situations and activities, and they illustrate the English that is useful in those circum-stances. While listening, you can, if you wish, read the Classroom Extract in the book.

Listening to the recording and repeating the teacher's part will help you to improve your own **intonation** and pronunciation and become more fluent. Studying the language used by proficient teachers (with the help of the written Classroom extracts) will help you to pick up useful classroom phrases as well as techniques for class control and management.

If you don't have a CD player, ask someone to copy the CD onto a C90 audiocassette for you (it is 75 minutes long). Then you can still make full use of the recordings.

What you get from each unit

Each unit begins with an **Overview** and an **Introduction** linking it to earlier units, and showing how the unit progresses.

This is followed by four to five **main sections**, each illustrating a different type of activity, for example, Listen and mime, Listen and colour.

Within each section there are normally some **sub-sections**:
— **An explanation, description, and/or rationale** is given for the activity type.
— **Classroom extracts** demonstrate the situation or activity being used in class. These are recorded on the CD and the written transcripts appear on the unit page.
— **Language Focus** exercises help you study aspects of the language from the classroom extracts, including stress and intonation. They also bring together sets of examples useful for daily classroom functions. You can record these on to your own personal audiocassette (see page 3).
— **Extension Ideas** list more activities of this kind or ways to extend them.
— **Teaching Tips** give ideas for adapting activities or setting them up differently.
— **Topic Talk** sections give you practice in talking about common topics with your classes, for example, families, animals, parties. This gives children a chance to listen to more English. Topic Talk often includes simple tasks that can be done on your own or with a friend or a colleague at work. We recommend that you record yourself doing the tasks on a separate audiocassette; then you can play it back and listen to yourself. The overall aim of Topic Talk is for you to become more fluent and confident in speaking in English in the classroom.
— **Pronunciation Points** focus on individual sounds that sometimes cause difficulty for learners and teachers. They are recorded on the CD. These points are for teachers only, not for children.

Each unit ends with a **Further Ideas** section with suggestions for follow-up reading and activities, things to try out in your classes or ways to plan materials.

Making the most of the CD

Wherever you see the 🎧 symbol, prepare to listen to the Classroom Extract. It is always more effective to listen more than once. In fact some teachers listen three or four times, each time for a different purpose. For example:

FIRST LISTENING
(preferably without reading the written extract)
— Try to understand in general what is happening in the lesson.

SECOND LISTENING
(again, possibly, without reading)
— Notice ways the teacher deals with particular situations.
— Notice stress and intonation patterns.

THIRD LISTENING
— Listen and read the Classroom extract in the book.
— Identify useful words and phrases used by the teacher.
— Try reading the teacher's part, out loud, in your own time, paying attention to intonation, stress, and pronunciation.

FOURTH LISTENING
— Practise by pausing the CD or cassette and repeating after the teacher, or by reading out loud, speaking along with the teacher.
— Identify words and phrases you need more practice with.
— Finally record yourself taking the teacher's part, and play it back to compare.

This whole process will help you to improve your pronunciation, gain fluency in speaking, and to acquire naturally many features of spontaneous classroom English.

NOTE
The CD is to help you to improve your own English, not to use in the classroom with children.

Recording yourself to build fluency and confidence

We know that as a teacher you do not have a lot of spare time, but we and our trainees have found that it is very useful to record yourself, on your own personal audiocassette, using some of the language from the extracts, tables, and exercises in that section. Play back your recording and see how you sound. If you are not satisfied, you can always erase your recording and try again.

Keep the recordings that you are happy with, and, after completing each unit, play them back and listen again. This is good revision and will help you recall useful expressions. To help you identify what you have recorded, record the unit and section number before starting.

However, before you record, practise! With the Language Focus activities, adapt the language to suit your own classes. Then, before recording, practise what you are going to say several times, trying out different intonation patterns. You can do the same with Topic Talk sections. You can also record yourself taking the teacher's part of the Classroom extracts, and then listen to the CD, to compare your pronunciation.

If you are lucky enough to have a friend or a colleague who speaks some English, or if you are on a course with other teachers, you could practise speaking with them. This would be especially helpful for sections like Topic Talk, or for storytelling. If you are on your own, then the process of recording yourself and listening as you play it back becomes even more vital for success. Do give it a try. It really does help you to remember the language you need and to speak English more easily.

We also suggest that you record yourself actually teaching in class, carrying out some of the activities from the unit. Later, play back your recording and listen to it once or twice to gain insights into your teaching and language use. A large number of teachers have already found that it helped them to improve their effectiveness. It can also help you focus on the children's progress.

From Unit 5 onwards, we help you to record some of your own teaching materials. So, to gain the most benefit from this book, you need to have two blank audiocassettes, one for personal language practice, and one to record teaching materials. Each time you see RECORD:
— *Read the instructions* and follow them carefully
— *Plan* what you could say
— *Practise* several different versions
— *Record yourself* on to your audiocassette
— *Play back*: listen, evaluate, and re-record if you wish to.

Using journals and portfolios to add to your learning experience

Some teachers have found it helpful to keep a *personal journal* while they are studying. After each study session, they write down in a notebook or personal journal what they have learnt or noticed from listening to their recordings, from trying things out in class, or ideas gained from reading or talking to pupils or colleagues. You can note down words and phrases you need to practise. Also, write any questions you have after each unit. Every two or three units, go back over and read what you have written, taking note of significant comments. You may even find answers to your own questions.

Other teachers put together a *portfolio of work*. For each unit, put into a folder or file ideas for new activities, materials for new stories (with visual aids), sample lesson outlines, and reports of lessons where you have tried out new ideas. You could also add an audiocassette, with recordings of yourself in class doing a selection of activities, or with materials for storytelling or listening activities. At the end of your course, you can select a number of your best pieces of work to make up a final portfolio, with title, name, and contents page. This final portfolio can be used
— to show new teachers what can be done
— to take to a job interview or to a training course
— to impress a visitor or an inspector
— for assessment purposes – some training courses and teachers' examining bodies now use final portfolios for end of course assessment.

Website

The Oxford Teacher's Club has a primary Website which includes:
— more examples of lessons and activities
— notes for teachers and course tutors
— opportunities for you to tell us what you think and send in your ideas.
Go to http://www.oup.co.uk/elt and click on 'Teacher's Club'.

A word about young learners

The activities suggested in the book are for a variety of ages and levels. Teaching situations differ all over the world, and children start English at different ages in different places, so we often suggest ways that activities can be adapted for older or younger children or for those with more or less English.

What are children like as learners?
They
— are developing quickly as individuals
— learn in a variety of ways, for example, by watching, by listening, by imitating, by doing things
— are not able to understand grammatical rules and explanations about language
— try to make sense of situations by making use of non-verbal clues
— talk in their mother tongue about what they understand and do – this helps them learn
— can generally imitate the sounds they hear quite accurately and copy the way adults speak
— are naturally curious
— love to play and use their imagination
— are comfortable with routines and enjoy repetition
— have quite a short attention span and so need variety.

How can you as teacher help them?
— Make learning English enjoyable and fun – remember you are influencing their attitude to language learning.
— Don't worry about mistakes. Be encouraging. Make sure children feel comfortable, and not afraid to take part.
— Use a lot of gestures, actions, pictures to demonstrate what you mean.
— Talk a lot to them in English, especially about things they can see.
— Play games, sing songs, say rhymes and chants together.
— Tell simple stories in English, using pictures and acting with different voices.
— Don't worry when they use their mother tongue. You can answer a mother tongue question in English, and sometimes recast in English what they say in their mother tongue.
— Constantly recycle new language but don't be afraid to add new things or to use words they won't know.
— Plan lessons with varied activities, some quiet, some noisy, some sitting, some standing and moving.

Because children show different characteristics at different ages, we sometimes make a distinction between very young learners (VYLs) aged under 7 years, and young learners (YLs) aged 7 to 12.

Teaching children under seven

If you are teaching a second language to children under seven, remember that very young learners:
— **acquire** through hearing and experiencing lots of English, in much the same way as they acquire their first language.
— learn through doing things and playing; they are not consciously trying to learn new words or phrases – for them this is incidental.
— love playing with language sounds, imitating and making funny noises. So have fun playing with words and phrases, for example, singing them, exaggerating your expression.
— are not able to organize their learning. Often they will not even realize that they are learning a foreign language. They simply see it as having fun!
— may not be able to read or write in their mother tongue, so it is important to recycle new words and expressions through talk and play.
— their grammar will develop gradually on its own, provided they hear lots of English and learn to understand a lot of words and phrases.

Teaching children between seven and twelve

Children from 7 to 12
— are learning to read and write in their
    own language
— are developing as thinkers
— understand the difference between the real
    and the imaginary
— can plan and organize how best to carry out
    an activity
— can work with others and learn from others
— can be reliable and take responsibility for class
    activities and routines.

When you are teaching 7–12 year olds you can
— encourage them to read in English (stories,
    comics, reading games)
— encourage them to work meanings out for
    themselves
— explain things about language, but only very
    simple things
— use a wider range of language input as their
    model for language use
— encourage creative writing and help them to
    experiment with language
— explain your intentions and ask them to help
    with organization of activities.
There will be more on these aspects in Unit 1.

We hope that you enjoy using this book and that you
will gain satisfaction from experimenting with new
ideas and trying out new language. Please let us
know (via the Website or publishers) how you get on
with this book, and if you have any suggestions for
improvements or additions.

We wish you and your learners well.

Mary Slattery, Dublin, Ireland
Jane Willis, Kendal, England

Introduction for trainers and tutors on courses

This book can be used as a basis for any training courses for teachers of English to 4–12 year olds.

We recommend that all tutors and teachers begin by reading carefully through the Introduction, as this gives insights into how the book was planned and advice on how to approach each section.

Recommendations for training sessions

There are some activities which would be best done in group sessions. Many activities denoted by the symbol ➲ will benefit participants more if done in pairs or small groups. On all training courses, there are some participants who feel shy and ashamed of their level of English, and who hesitate to speak English in front of the whole group. In the relative privacy of a small group or pair, they are less likely to worry about making mistakes and are more likely to try out new words and phrases. Working in pairs increases the opportunities they get for spontaneous speech, and helps them develop their fluency and confidence.

Starting a new section
Begin each new section by letting participants read the rationale for the activity type, and then summarize and/or discuss the main points either as a class or with participants in groups.

Using the CD and the classroom extracts
A CD is provided with this book because it gives teachers examples of English in use in the classroom. It is the simplest and most direct way to show how listening to English can improve pronunciation and intonation.

Before playing the CD, ensure teachers understand the classroom context. As you progress through the book, you may get to know some of the teachers on the CD quite well. Note that some of the teachers contributed several lessons at different levels. You may need to explain to participants that the original teachers' recordings had to be re-recorded by actors in a studio, which is why some teachers sound rather similar to each other. (Reassure them that the actors had heard the original tapes and kept as close as possible to the original.)

In the session, you may need to play the CD more than once. Ideas for what to focus on each time are given in the section itself and there are more ideas in the main Introduction. Participants might profit from some choral repetition of short chunks and phrases, to focus on stress and intonation, as well as pronunciation of key words.

In the Language Focus sections we have focused on certain aspects of language used in the lesson extract. Participants could, however, analyse other aspects of an extract.

TEACHING TIPS: participants can read through the tips and relate them to their own experience. Then in pairs or groups they can
— tell others about their own experience of similar techniques, situations ('I once did/used … with a class of eight year olds …')
— suggest situations in their classes where such tips might help, and say how they might actually carry them out
— give ideas for adapting the tips or setting activities up differently.
After this, ask some pairs to report their best idea to the class. Give the whole group time to prepare what to say, if they are asked.

EXTENSION IDEAS: participants read through these ideas, then
— choose one they have experience of, or would like to try out, and tell each other what they did/might do in class and what the good things/difficulties were/might be
— try to suggest another similar activity, or another topic this could be done with
— think of ways to extend them further, and add reading or writing activities.
After this, ask some different pairs to report their best idea to the class. Again, give the whole class time to prepare what to say.

Language Focus exercises
These can be done in pairs. Encourage participants to
— add to and adapt the language in the tables (explaining to each other in what context their phrases would be used) and then practise in pairs

— do the task (for example, pairing, adding, sequencing, spotting the odd one out) first on their own and then compare the way they did it with their partner, reading the phrases out loud.

Let participants try out some short interactions, role-playing with each other, and building on the examples a little more. Encourage them to

— exaggerate the intonation and expression they use while doing this, for fun
— say the phrases/examples out loud from memory, without reading them from the book
— see how many they can remember in one minute without looking back at the book
— choose the most useful language and tell the class what it was and when they could use it
— write new words and expressions in their language notebooks
— prepare together in pairs what they are going to record on their personal cassette at home.

During the following session, ask participants if you can hear a short sample from some of their recordings. (Participants can choose what bit to play to the class, and have their cassettes wound back, ready to play, at the start of the session.) This is a good way of ensuring that participants actually do make the effort to record. And always think of something positive to say about their contributions.

We emphasize getting participants to record themselves because we believe that 'going public' greatly enhances the desire to improve their own language, and the effort put into preparing for the recording aids both memory retention and recall.

Topic Talk and Storytelling

These are best done in small groups, to increase opportunities for teacher talk. Topic Talk sections are set up differently in each unit on purpose to give teachers experience of a variety of types of interaction and activity. See the main Introduction for further rationale. You may well wish to change or supplement these topics to suit your local syllabus.

If your participants need more fluency practice and opportunities for sustained talk, ask them to prepare a simple story on a familiar topic, to tell in the next group session. They can do this even before they get to the units on storytelling. You can set a one-minute time limit to begin with. Sometimes they can record their story in their own time and play it back in a group session. If they are shy, they can tell or play their story in small groups of three or four.

Follow-up presentations

After pair or group discussions of Extension Ideas, Teaching Tips, and Topic Talk, participants can be asked to present their findings or best ideas to another small group or to the whole class. Because this constitutes a more 'public' performance, there will be a natural urge to be as accurate and as organized as possible. But before they present their findings in public, they will benefit from some planning time, when they plan roughly what they will say and try to make their language suitably accurate. During this planning time, they can ask a trainer if they are not sure of a language point, or check in a dictionary or with their co-participants.

This process mirrors a three-part Task-based approach (Willis 1996):

TASK
— done in pairs or small groups
— spontaneous talk
   (mistakes don't matter).

PLANNING
— pairs decide what ideas to present to the whole group
— efforts made to plan appropriate language that is both fluent and accurate.

REPORT
— tutor asks some pairs/groups to report their ideas, i.e. to present their ideas to the whole class
— this is more formal planned talk
— the ideas can then be summarized or discussed.

Further study ideas

Here we would like to encourage teachers to continue in their own personal self-development. Many of the ideas ask teachers to look back again at specific activities and language, to listen again to extracts, and then to plan, work out, and write down ideas for lessons. Then finally teachers can try out their ideas, teach, and record their own classes.

Teachers could keep a record in their journals of any comments or analysis, and the self-evaluation they are doing. Using journals helps trainees structure their own learning and become more aware of their specific needs.

You might find it useful to make notes on some of the things you learn from looking at their journals, if you have agreed beforehand that you can read them.

Organizing teaching practice activities with a focus on classroom language

The following pattern has proved useful for practising classroom language in training sessions. It could be used with the activities or situations illustrated in a classroom extract, or suggested in a Teaching Tips or Extension Ideas section.

Divide participants into groups of three (or possibly four, but not less than three).

Ask them to appoint one teacher, one or two children, and one language secretary.

— Tell and show the 'teachers' from each group what they have to do.
— Tell the 'children' from each group that they must *only* do what they are actually told by the teacher, and nothing else. (As teachers they may see in advance the point of activities and may do what they know is required, not just what the 'teacher' says.)
— Tell the language secretaries to write down as much as they can of what the 'teacher' says. Some groups could use a tape recorder if conditions allow this.

When the activity is finished each group can analyse their performance in terms of language used with the help of a form like the following:

Participants' names _____

Language used for activity	What was clear and why	What was unclear and why	How to improve

Each time you do this let different participants role-play the teacher, the children, and language secretary. When all the groups have finished they can pool their findings and see what they have learnt.

This kind of group activity should help teachers support one another and help them feel less nervous about teaching in front of larger groups.

Contact time on training courses is often limited. You may want to ask course participants to read and study some parts of each unit on their own. They can write down in their own language notebook any new language they see or questions they have, to ask you in class.

Recommendations for individual study during a course

a in preparation for course sessions, as introductory reading, participants could:
   — read the Introduction to the book
   — read the outline contents and introduction to each unit
   — read the beginnings of sections where some rationale is given
   — prepare some ideas for Topic Talk or storytelling.

b as a follow-up to course sessions, for language consolidation purposes, participants could:
   — listen to the classroom extracts on the CD again
   — practise their personal pronunciation and intonation using the CD
   — record themselves and play back their recordings
   — prepare to talk about activities that they have done with their own learners.

c for preparing class activities and teaching practice sessions, and keeping records:
   — prepare new activities to try out in class or in group sessions
   — write their journal and keep up a language notebook
   — keep a record of successful activities and teaching materials for a portfolio.

At the end of the course

Encourage teachers to form local support groups so they continue to have the opportunity to compare and discuss teaching ideas with colleagues. After the training session they may arrange to meet occasionally or regularly, and to share ideas and materials.

1 Teaching young learners

This unit looks at

- how children **acquire** their first language
- how we can help children acquire English as a second language
- opportunities for using English when starting lessons, changing activities, and ending lessons
- the differences between teaching young learners and very young learners.

1.1 First language – second language

Knowing how children learn their first language can help us teach them a second language.

All children can speak at least one language when they come to school. Think about how they learn this first language. Think about babies and young children. Most mothers talk a lot to their children.

Babies

— hear voices from the time they are born
— respond to the voices of their mother, father, or carer
— listen to a lot of sound
— play with sounds and practise making sounds
— begin to associate the sounds with what they can see and understand
— begin to use language to interact with others and get what they want.

Young children

— say what they hear others saying
— pick up the accent of those around them.

Read this transcript of a mother talking to her little child of 16 months. Notice how much language she uses and how she talks about what is happening to the child.

⊶ **a** How many phrases does she actually say? And how many words does the child say?

MOTHER: Now we're nearly dressed … OK now over your head … good boy … put in your other hand … now shoes. Where are your shoes?
CHILD: Sus …
MOTHER: Yes. Your shoes. Where are they?
    (*Both look around for the shoes.*)
MOTHER: Oh there. Look … your shoes … on the chair.
CHILD: Sus. Sus.
MOTHER: Yes shoes.

1A

Thinking about the Easter Bunny and eliciting the phrase *chocolate eggs*

TEACHER: And it's a holiday, isn't it?

CHILDREN: Yeah.

TEACHER: Yes. And on Easter Sunday he brings us what? Em?

CHILDREN: Chocolate.

TEACHER: Chocolate? Uh uh chocolate. Eh, chocolate … ice-cream?

CHILDREN: No.

TEACHER: No, no it's not chocolate ice-cream. Eh … chocolate … eggs? Chocolate eggs. Yes?

CHILDREN: Yes.

TEACHER: Do you like chocolate eggs?

CHILDREN: Yes, yes.

TEACHER: Mm … Yum yum yum, yes?

CHILDREN: Yes, yes.

TEACHER: Chocolate eggs. OK.
(*later in the class*)

TEACHER: And he brings? He brings? Yes?

CHILD: Chocolate eggs.

TEACHER: Do you like chocolate eggs? Do you like chocolate eggs? I love chocolate eggs.

Clara with eight to nine year olds.

This kind of talk is called **caretaker talk**; parents as carers talk to help the development of their child's language.

Teachers in school can do the same with their learners. Think about young children learning English as a second language when they go to school.

Young children will
— only acquire the language they hear around them
— need to hear a lot of English
— look on you – their teacher – as their new carer
— listen to you and try to make sense of what you say
— sound like the people they listen to.

Listen to the teacher in **1A** talking to her class about the Christian festival of Easter. It is important in many Western countries. Children have holidays and get chocolate eggs.

Although the topic is quite different from the mother dressing her child, she uses language in similar ways. Look at the transcripts and try to find two similarities.

LANGUAGE FOCUS 1.1

Caretaker talk

The conversation between the mother and the young child and classroom extract **1A** are similar in many ways.
— Firstly, both mother and teacher talk a lot more than the children do.
— Secondly, they provide a secure and supportive environment which gives the children confidence to try out language.

b Look at the table below. Find examples of four other similarities and complete this table.

What the teacher/parent does	Mother–child	Teacher–child
Repeats phrases said earlier.	M: Now shoes … Yes your shoes. Look … your shoes	1
Keeps children's attention by asking them questions.	2	T: And he brings us what? He brings? He brings?
Reacts positively to what children say even if words are not complete or perfectly pronounced.	CH: Sus – Sus M: Yes, shoes	3
Adds to or improves what children say.	4	CH: Chocolate eggs. T: Do you like chocolate eggs?

These features of caretaker talk can help learners acquire new language naturally. So they are very good things for teachers to do when teaching English in class.

Which of them do you do already?

🎧 Pronunciation point
Syllables

⊶ Sounds /ʧ/ and /ʃ/

1 Say the word *chocolate*. How many syllables are you pronouncing in this word?

    Some words, like *chocolate*, have syllables that are written but are often dropped when people speak.

    What about these words? *every, different, favourite, comfortable, vegetable*.

2 Which of the <u>underlined</u> sounds in these words is the odd-one-out? *cho<u>c</u>olate, <u>ch</u>ildren, <u>ch</u>eck, <u>sh</u>oulders, tea<u>ch</u>er, pic<u>t</u>ure*.

TEACHING TIPS

Helping children learn a new language

- ✔ Use English in class as the main language for communication.
- ✔ Use **gestures**, actions, and pictures to help children understand.
- ✔ Children often need to talk in order to learn – let children use their mother tongue for communication, especially to start with.
- ✔ **Recast** in English what children say to you in their mother tongue.
- ✔ Answer children in English as much as possible.

- ✔ Use their mother tongue for support when you do a new activity or if no one understands.
- ✔ Talk a lot in English to your pupils – they need to hear English.
  Talk about
  — where things are
  — pictures or things children can see
  — what you and your pupils are doing in class
  — what you want your pupils to do next.

REMEMBER
— The more English the children hear, the more they will learn.
— They will learn gradually – they won't say everything perfectly to start with. Encourage them by responding positively.

1B

Greetings

TEACHER: Good morning.
CHILDREN: Morning, teacher.
TEACHER: How are you today?
CHILDREN: Very well. How are you?
TEACHER: Fine. Thanks.

Clara with eight to nine year olds.

1C

A question of routine

TEACHER: Good morning. Is today Monday?
CHILDREN: No.
TEACHER: Or maybe Tuesday? Or Sunday?
CHILDREN: No.
TEACHER: Oh I wish it was Sunday. OK, what day is it today?
CHILDREN: Thursday.
TEACHER: Great!

Cristina with nine to ten year olds.

1.2   Starting your lessons in English

To help your children acquire English, speak English from the beginning of each English lesson. What you say then will, of course, depend on whether you are their everyday class teacher, or whether you are a specialist English teacher.

Are you a class teacher?

A class teacher teaches every subject, including English, to the same class. Your pupils are listening to you, the class teacher, all day. Think about how you start your English lessons. Write down two or three things you might say or do to make sure they know it is English next.

Are you a specialist teacher?

A specialist teacher only teaches English but usually teaches several classes. You might work with pupils of different ages and levels. Think about what you say to the children in these different classes when you begin your lesson. Write down three or four things you might say in English, or things you might do.

1D

Calling the roll in English

TEACHER: OK, let's check the roll. Now, remember to answer, 'I'm here'.
TEACHER: Giupone, Lorenzo.
LORENZO: I'm here.
TEACHER: Pierrotti, Jonathan.
(silence)
CHILDREN: Not here.
TEACHER: What about Jonathan. Where is he? 'I don't know'. Can you say that?
CHILDREN: (repeating) I don't know.
TEACHER: OK, everyone's here except Jonathan.

Clara with eight to nine year olds.

1E

Starting with a song

TEACHER: Morning.
CHILDREN: Morning.
TEACHER: OK. Can you stand up now? Please. OK, Amanda can you stand up too? Thank you. OK, let's sing a song. But do you remember how to put your hands on your heads? Yes? Like this.
(Teacher puts his hands on his head.)
TEACHER: OK, do you remember this song? OK … Head and shoulders, knees and toes …
(All sing together)

Juan with eight to nine year olds.

🎧 Listen to the teachers in extracts **1B** to **1E** starting their English lessons. Look at the things you have written down. Do any of these teachers
— do what you do?
— say what you say?

🎧 Listen again to extracts **1B** to **1E**. Pause after any useful **phrases** and repeat them, paying special attention to the intonation.

RECORD Record yourself taking the teacher's part in some of these extracts. Then play your recording back and compare with the original. Re-record if you like.

LANGUAGE FOCUS 1.2

Greetings and forms of address

Addressing a teacher by name is usual in some countries, whereas in others children use the word *Teacher* as a title. What happens in your country? Practise some suitable phrases from this table.

Teacher		Children	
Good morning,	children.	Good morning,	Miss/Mrs/Mr/Ms [surname].
Good afternoon,	everybody.	Good afternoon,	[first name].
Hello,	boys and girls.	Hello,	Teacher.
	girls and boys.		

Checking attendance

↻ Think how you could have a small conversation with your children as well as calling their names. Practise, using the tables below and then add to these conversations by using the ideas under the tables.

RECORD Record two possible conversations.

Let's call the roll. Let's take the register. Let's check to see who is here.	Thank you, everybody.
Remember to answer 'I'm here'.	So, everyone is here except … So, only two people away.

Is everybody here?	Oh good, Paula, you're back. Nice to see you. Are you all right now?	
Is anyone away? No-one absent today? Who is missing?	Oh, John's away. Who knows why? Is he ill?	Maybe he's gone to the dentist. What do you think?
Let's all count to see if everyone is here – girls first, then boys.	So, how many is 13 and 15? OK … Yes? So that is 28 altogether.	Is that more than yesterday? Or less than yesterday? Or the same?

Ways of starting lessons

↻ Look at the ideas below. Choose some of the things you might do, and write in the bubble what you might say. Two examples have been done for you. Add more ideas if you can. Practise saying them out loud, slowly then quickly.

Is everybody here?
Is anyone away/missing?
No? OK, so let's start.

check attendance

sing a song

do question routines,
e.g. days of the week,
the weather, birthdays

take the register/
call the roll

We need some more space
for today's lesson – you
there – can you help me
move some tables back.

rearrange the classroom

say a rhyme

play a game

RECORD   Then record the phrases you might find useful.

TEACHING TIPS

Class Teachers

✔ Do something different so that everyone knows it's time for English, e.g. sing a special song.
✔ Wear something special during the lesson, e.g. a badge, a hat …
✔ Stand in a different place or arrange the room differently.
✔ Put up a picture or get out toys that children associate with English.

Specialist Teachers

✔ Plan something familiar in English at the beginning of the lesson to make the change of teacher easier.
✔ Use a special name chart to check who's present.
✔ Prepare a **routine** that the children like, e.g. sing a song or say a rhyme.

Monday Tuesday Wednesday – Hop!
Thursday Friday Saturday – Shop!
Sunday – take a rest and – Flop!

1.3   Organizing your classroom

Think of all the things you might say to your classes in your mother tongue during the day when you are organizing your class. Write down three or four of these sentences in English, for example, *Turn your chairs around and face the clock.*

🎧 Listen to extracts **1F** to **1H**. Notice how the teachers talk in short **chunks**, one phrase at a time. Listen for the **key word(s)** in each phrase – the words that carry the main stress. These words carry the main message.

1F

Arranging the classroom

TEACHER: Now, you four Peter, Paula, Tony, and Ann. Move the tables back without making a noise. OK, leave these five tables here at the top.
    OK, any more left? Right, we're nearly ready. OK, everyone listen, listen, don't move these desks, OK …

Cristina with nine to ten year olds.

1G

Changing from one activity to another

TEACHER: OK, now, now put everything away. We're going to do something else. We're going to do something else. OK now … sh … sh … sh … quietly …

Jane with seven to eight year olds.

1H

Asking and giving permission

TEACHER: Have you finished? Everybody finished?
DANIEL: Teacher, Teacher …
TEACHER: What do you want Daniel?
DANIEL: May I go to the toilet please?
TEACHER: Yes, OK, but no one else. Wait for the break.

Emi with eleven to twelve year olds.

a Listen again and <u>underline</u> them.

RECORD   Now choose one of the extracts **1F–1H** which you like and repeat the teacher's part, using the same **intonation**.

LANGUAGE FOCUS 1.3

Everyday instructions – organizing the classroom

b Listen to the three extracts **1F–1H** again. Which teacher repeats and which two teachers **rephrase** a part of their instructions?
    Now read the following ten instructions out loud.

1 Get your books and pencils out.
2 Pick your pencils up.
3 Move the tables back.
4 Turn your chairs round to face the wall chart.
5 Put all your things away.
6 Close the window beside you.
7 Put your pencils down.
8 Turn back to face the front.
9 Leave these tables here.
10 Leave the windows open.

c For each instruction, find one which has the opposite meaning. There are five pairs of opposites.

d Nine of these instructions contain phrases that end with an adverb or adjective, like *back* or *open*. Read these out loud with a slight **stress** on the adverb, and notice the similarities in rhythm.

➲ What words or phrases might you add *before* these instructions to get your children's attention? For example, *OK, all of you, get your books and pencils out.*
    To get some ideas, look at the classroom extracts in the boxes above and below. Practise saying your longer versions out loud, as if you were in front of a class.
    How else might you adapt these instructions for your class/es?

Play around with them and see how many small changes you can make to each one, to suit children of different levels. For example

Put all your things back in your bags.
Right, can you put everything away now?
You don't need to move these desks; they are fine as they are.

Practise saying your new instructions as if to learners of different ages or levels.

RECORD   Choose around seven useful instructions to record on your cassette.

1.4 Ending your lessons

What do your children normally do after your English lesson?
Do they
— stay in the same room?
— go to another lesson in a different room?
— have a break?
— go home?
How do you normally finish your lessons? What might you say?
Write down three things.

🎧   Now listen to extracts 1I and 1J, and compare what these teachers do and say with your own ideas.

🎧   Listen again and imitate their intonation patterns. Repeat any phrases you find useful.

1I

Ending a lesson

TEACHER: Right, we have no time for anything else. Don't do any more. We don't have any more time today …

Cristina with seven to eight year olds.

1J

Finishing up

TEACHER: That's all for today. OK, on Monday there will be more. OK, OK, now children, now, make a line to say good bye … following the leader …

Juan with six to seven year olds.

LANGUAGE FOCUS 1.4

Ending lessons

Read the examples below. They all come from real lessons.

1   OK, that's all for <u>now</u>.
2   Right. We've no time for anything else – don't do any more – we don't have any more time <u>today</u>.

3 OK – just one more time before going <u>out for a short break</u>.
4 OK, now stop! We haven't enough time to finish <u>the monster</u> today.
   So stand up…
5 OK – just <u>one more time</u> – and then that's it.
6 OK, pick up all your things – and put the books <u>in the cupboard</u>.
7 That's all for today. On <u>Monday</u>, there'll be more.
8 OK, children, make a line to say good-bye – <u>following the leader</u>. Bye bye.
9 OK, it's <u>break-time</u>. So you can go out to play. But first – line up quietly by
   the door.

a Find four pairs of phrases that have similar meanings. Read them out loud
in pairs.

b In each example, one word or a phrase is <u>underlined</u>. Change or substitute
this one word or phrase for another word or phrase, for example, change
<u>now</u> to <u>this afternoon</u>.

RECORD Practise saying them out loud and then record yourself.

Phrases with *else*

c Read **1G**, **1H** and **1I** again and find whole phrases that go with *no one else,
something else, anything else* and practise them. Can you think of two other
common classroom phrases with *else*?

Word quiz

d *Now – OK – Right – OK now –*
What three things do these words and phrases have in common? Think
of where they are used, how they are said, what their classroom function is.

RECORD Look back at the classroom extracts in this unit and write down and record
on your cassette any more useful phrases you could use.

TEACHING TIPS

Using English for class organization

✔ While preparing your lesson, make a
list of classroom language for each
activity.
✔ Prepare to say all of this in English
during the lesson.
✔ Use songs and rhymes when you
change from one activity to another,
e.g. an action song to start a game.

✔ Encourage your pupils to use English
for routine classroom requests by
praising any effort they make.
✔ Use wall charts or posters to help
children remember what you are
doing in the English class.

1.5 Very Young Learners (VYLs) and Young Learners (YLs)

↻ Do you teach very young learners aged seven and under or young
learners aged seven and over? What are the major differences? List three.
Read the section on VYLs and YLs in the Introduction (pages 4–5) again
and tick the points that are relevant to your situation.
Now compare how the children react in the next two extracts,
1K and **1L**.

1 K

Very young learners listening to a story

TEACHER: Are they happy? Are they
happy? Yes, they are laughing…
CHILD: Happy, happy, happy…
TEACHER: Yes, and are they laughing?
CHILD: Laughing, laughing, laughing…

Susan with six to seven year olds.

1 L

Young learners guessing from visual clues

TEACHER: Now I'm going to talk to you about a new person. Can anyone tell me who this is?

CHILD: A man.

CHILD: A person.

TEACHER: Yes, yes. A small person or a big person?

CHILD: Small … big … small …

TEACHER: OK, this is not a normal person. Who do you think it is?

CHILD: A child.

TEACHER: Look carefully … let's take out a bit more …

(*There is lots of mother tongue talk as all the children try to guess – one child says in his mother tongue 'a snowman'.*)

TEACHER: Yes. It's a snowman and look … I'm going to show you his face. Look … he has a carrot for a nose. What colour is the carrot?

CHILD: Orange.

TEACHER: This is a very nice snowman. Now before I take him out, look at his face. Is he a big snowman or a little snowman?

CHILD: Middle … middle …

TEACHER AND PUPILS: Middle sized.

TEACHER: OK, now listen.

Cristina with eight to nine year olds.

🎧 The first teacher is telling a story to children under seven. They are making sense of the story with the help of the pictures. Some children are imitating the teacher – repeating naturally what she is saying, and looking at the pictures.

🎧 Now listen to the next teacher, Cristina, with a group of eight and nine year olds. She is slowly taking a drawing out of an envelope. The children can only see a small part of the figure and they are trying to guess what it is. Compared to the very young learners, they are more aware of answering and recalling the words they need when she asks them a question.

Notice how the teacher allows the children to talk in their mother tongue (MT) and when she hears a child say something relevant in MT she immediately recasts it in English. What word does she recast in this transcript?

LANGUAGE FOCUS 1.5

Telling the class what you are doing

The teacher in **1L** builds up the children's natural curiosity by pulling out the picture very slowly.

a Can you find three or four places where she tells the class what she is doing or about to do? Read them, then say each one out loud, from memory, slowly then quickly.

Asking questions

Can you find five questions and repeat them with the same intonation that she used?

b Which two questions are very similar?

TEACHING TIPS

Very young learners

✔ Introduce English slowly with enjoyable activities.

✔ Support what you say with gestures, actions, movements, and facial expression.

✔ Help the children feel secure by repeating familiar activities, e.g. songs and rhymes.

✔ Repeat in English what children say to you in their mother tongue.

✔ Use a puppet to talk to in English. Tell the children the puppet can only speak English so they have to speak in English to the puppet. If a child speaks in his/her mother tongue to the puppet, you can recast and speak to the puppet.

✔ Use drawings and photos.

✔ Tell lots of stories using pictures for support.

Young learners

Adapt the approaches you use with VYLs, and in addition

✔ Explain in mother tongue on the first day why you are using English during the English lesson.

✔ Teach the class useful phrases about language use, e.g. *Can I use … (mother tongue)? What's … in English?*

✔ Plan for success and a positive experience.

✔ Talk about your own personal experiences, e.g. What you like/dislike. This is like telling stories.

And above all, have fun!

TOPIC TALK
Introducing yourself

If you are beginning a course or starting a class with new people, they will probably want to know something about you. How much you say and what you say will of course depend on who these people are – fellow teachers on a course, or pupils in a class. And the age and level of the pupils also makes a difference.

First, think of a possible audience. Think how you might introduce yourself to them.

↩ Here are some ideas to start you off. Select ideas that are suitable for your audience, and adapt and expand them. Practise putting some of them together to make a short personal **presentation**.

RECORD Then record it and play it back and listen to it. Re-record if you want to improve it.

My name is _____ but you can call me _____.

I've been working at _____ school for _____ years, and like it/the pupils very much.

So what are my interests, apart from teaching? Well, I enjoy _____.
Another thing I like doing is _____ but it is very expensive!

Shall I tell you about some of my favourite things? As far as food goes, what I like best is _____ and _____. On television, I always watch _____.

And as for the future, one of my dreams/ambitions is to _____. I'd really like that!

Further ideas

1 Buy a notebook to use for your private study. You could use this as a diary while you are following this course.

2 Play back and listen to the useful phrases you recorded while doing Unit 1. Start using them in class.

3 Plan a lesson where you hope to use as much English as possible. Work out what you can say in English at different stages in the lesson. Teach the lesson and see how it goes. Write down your reactions.

4 Take a cassette recorder with microphone into your next class. Record the first ten minutes of your lesson. Listen to it two or three times. In your notebook write down what you notice about your class. Think about the things you said and did. Answer the following questions:
— How much English did you speak in the first ten minutes? 20%? 50%? 70%? More?
— Did you switch to your mother tongue at all? When and why?
— What did you use your mother tongue for? Can you now think of phrases in English that would be suitable? Write these down.
— Did you notice yourself using any **caretaker talk**? Did you miss any opportunities for caretaker talk?

5 Read Chapters 1 and 2 from:
Lightbown, Patsy M. and Nina Spada. 1999. *How Languages are Learned* (second edition). Oxford: Oxford University Press.

2

Listen and do

Introduction

If you ask children in English to do something you are
— using language for a purpose
— giving them the opportunity to show they understand.
Your pupils need to understand just enough to follow your instructions, but they don't need to speak yet. Each time you speak in English you are giving your pupils another opportunity
— to acquire the language
— to absorb the sounds and patterns of the language naturally.
The teachers you will hear in this unit are carrying out a selection of 'listen and do' activities in English. These activities could be part of almost any lesson.
    Let's look, first of all, at the kind of basic instructions you use every day
— in between teaching activities
— when organizing your children.

2.1 Giving instructions in English

It is very easy to use your mother tongue when asking children to sit, stand, or move around in preparation for another activity. It is often easier and quicker. But your aim is to teach them English, not to be quick. At first, while telling them what to do in English, you can use gestures and demonstrate what you want them to do. After a few days, they will understand without your gestures, and they will have learnt a lot more English.

LANGUAGE FOCUS 2.1

Look at the **phrases** on the next page. Choose the ones you might use in your lessons.

⊃ Make any changes you need to. Practise saying the phrases with suitable gestures.

RECORD Finally, choose around ten to record on your own cassette.

Sitting down and standing up

Come in please and sit down.
    OK– sit down now please.
    Sit down together at your tables.
    OK– everyone – sit down – quietly.
    Ana – sit down over there – with
your friend.

Midori, turn round and face the front.
    OK, everybody, stop talking now and
listen carefully.

OK, please stand up. And don't make too
much noise.
    Everybody up! That's right!

Stand still! Don't move.
    Stay in your places! Stay where
you are.

Moving around

Right, Taro, can you come here, please?
    OK, come out here to the front of
the class.
    OK, your group, come up to the front.
    Right, now, you, you, and you … come
over here.

Now, get into a line. Stand in a line.
    I want you to make two lines, along
here …
    Like this … one behind the other.
    Let's see … move up a bit … good …
that's nice and straight!

Can you make a circle? A nice round
circle. Good!
    Not too close … a bit further apart …
step back a bit, that's better!
    Suresh … come forward a bit … Yes,
that's it.

OK, thank you. Now go back to
your places.

2.2 Listening and identifying

When children do 'listen and identify' activities they are
— practising a basic language skill – listening
— making sense of English words and phrases
— developing their vocabulary
— acquiring meaning and sound together.

For vocabulary development

For 'listen and identify' activities you can use:
— the classroom and all the things the children can see, such as wall
   charts, pictures, and picture cards
— **Cuisenaire rods** or coloured bricks or blocks for colour words or size words
— objects that you/children bring in, for example, things to eat such as
   fruit, biscuits, sweets; sets of farm animals, other small toys
— objects that children draw or make from paper, plasticine, or other
   craft materials.

There are generally two stages to 'listen and identify' activities.
1 Talk to the children about the things you want them to learn the
    names of:
    Look, here's my bag. Now, what have I got in here?
    There's a book, that's my English book …
    And my pencil box, with my pencils in it …
    Look … I'll open it.
    Here are my pencils … some coloured pencils.
    One, two, three, four pencils …
2 Ask the children to point to or show you the things when you
    name them.

2 A

Personal possessions

TEACHER: OK now … show me your book, your book. Show me your book that's in your bag. Where's your book? (*Children take out books – lots of mother tongue talk.*)

TEACHER: OK. Good. Now show me your pencil box … your pencil box … your pencil box. Show me your pencil box. Let me see your pencil box. Good. One, two, three, good. Your pencil box? Good.

Erin with four to five year olds.

2 B

Listen and point

TEACHER: OK, OK. Listen carefully. OK. One, two, three. Are you ready, OK, steady, let's go. Point to the picture I am talking about. Is it the boy or the girl?

He's wearing a blue sweater, right. He's wearing a blue sweater. (*The children point*) Yes, very good. It's the boy … OK. Now, she's carrying a green schoolbag. She's carrying a green schoolbag. …

Brian with seven to eight year olds.

Listen to the teacher in **2A** at the second stage with her very young learners. The children are identifying what she is calling out. They do this a lot and it is like a game that they play.

Notice how this teacher
— changes her language as she asks the children to show her different things
— repeats a lot
— sings some phrases
— keeps everything moving quite fast.

The important thing for these very young learners is to listen and identify. They are associating what they have in their hands with the phrases the teacher is using.

You can also use
— small picture cards which they can hold up and show you
— big pictures on the wall or other classroom objects, and the children can point to what you call out.

Later on, children may begin to repeat the words and then you can encourage them to practise saying them.

For grammatical awareness

You can use 'listen and identify' activities to do more than extend the children's vocabulary. For example, with older learners, you can help them to distinguish between
— singular and plural, by pointing to cards with one or more items on: *A dog. Some dogs. It's brown. They are brown.*
— gender pronouns, by pointing at cards with different people on them. You don't teach grammar to very young learners but you can help them discover meanings. By doing activities that focus on basic **concepts** such as singular/plural or gender, children unconsciously begin to acquire a feeling for what is grammatically **accurate**. (This does not mean that they will get it right every time they speak!)

For this kind of activity you could also use fun pictures of cartoon characters or pictures from story books but the original meaning must be clear.

Now listen to the teacher in **2B**. He has put two pictures on the board. One is a picture of a boy. It is on the left. The other is a picture of a girl. It is on the right.

They are both alike, both wearing the same colours, carrying the same schoolbags, doing the same things. But there are a few differences.

The teacher wants the children
— to listen carefully and point to the correct picture when they hear *she* or *he*
— to associate the pronouns *he* and *she* with gender
— to **absorb** where colour adjectives come in English.

He repeats what he says at natural speed and with natural intonation.

LANGUAGE FOCUS 2.2

Being good – a positive approach to discipline

How can you get young children to settle down and listen properly? Here are some things you can say in order to control children but still sound positive and encourage good behaviour.

— *Please stop talking now. No more talking for a bit. Good, you lot. That is nice and quiet. You others … sh … sh. Calm down now, OK. That's better.*
— *Quiet please! Settle down now and listen. That's good, Eva. Thank you, Emilio.*
— *Everyone is sitting really nicely … except for Tom! Tom, could you sit down like the others please? Thank you. OK …*
— *OK, we need to be quieter to hear what everyone is saying. These two groups are doing an excellent job. Thank you for being quiet. And now we are waiting for …*
— *Now who can tell me the name of the book. Lots of hands raised. Excellent.*

↻ Imagine when you might use these or similar phrases with your pupils. Adapt these examples to suit your situation, then practise them.

RECORD Record three examples on your cassette.

🎧 Pronunciation point

○⇥ **Sounds /s/, /k/, and /ʃ/**
1 Say these twelve words: *pencil, special, face, fantastic, carrying, carefully, combing, dice, ocean, ceiling, physical, bouncy.*
2 You pronounce the letter *c* in three different ways: /s/, /k/, and /ʃ/. Group the words according to the sound of *c* in each word.

2.3 Listening and doing – Total Physical Response

Total Physical Response (TPR) is when children listen and follow a whole sequence of instructions, doing what the teacher says. It is a good way to start using English for communication in the classroom.

The teacher
— tells the pupils what to do
— uses clear pronunciation and natural intonation
— helps them understand by gestures or by doing the actions.

The pupils
— have to listen carefully to the instructions
— enjoy doing the actions
— can do the actions all together or on their own
— do not have to speak (but often do!)
— understand because the movement and language go together.

Here are some TPR activities.

Follow the leader

The most basic TPR is when children copy the teacher and listen to what
she says.

Listen to the teacher in **2C**. It is her first class. She is playing 'follow the
leader'. All the children get in line behind the teacher. The children follow
her and copy her movements.

2 C

Follow the leader

TEACHER: OK, now get in a line. Peter …
you're here. Now Anna. Now Lara.
   OK, now follow me. Come on …
round the class. OK, we're walking,
walking, walking. Now, jumping like
a kangaroo, jumping, jumping. Yes.
Now flying … like a plane. We're
flying, flying, flying … down again.
We're driving … driving on the bus …
driving …

Lucy with six to seven year olds.

'Follow the leader' is a good activity for very young learners starting to
learn English. It is good fun and they see and understand what to do at
the same time. Later, when children are familiar with the activity, they
can take turns calling out the instructions to the others.

Topic-based TPR

You can use TPR activities for vocabulary practice.

Listen to the teacher in **2D**. She is practising clothes vocabulary and
simple movements.
   You could do something similar to practise colours: *If you are wearing
something blue, put your hand up … If you've got on something green,
stand on one leg …*

TPR routines

You can use TPR to wake children up if they are feeling sleepy, or let
children have a break when they have been concentrating on another
activity.

2 D

TPR with clothes vocabulary

TEACHER: Now … listen carefully.
Now everyone who's wearing jeans …
stand up.
   (*Child wearing jeans stands up.*)
TEACHER: OK. Good. Now … Now, if you
are wearing a T- shirt, come up here.

Lucy with seven to eight year olds.

2 E

An action routine

TEACHER: Clap your hands.
  Clap your hands.
  Slap your legs.
  Slap your legs.
  Stamp your feet.
  Stamp your feet.
  Snap your fingers.
  Snap your fingers.
  Clap your hands.
  Clap your hands.

Juan with eight to nine year olds.

2 F

A pointing rhyme

TEACHER: Point to the ceiling.
  Point to the floor.
  Point to the window.
  Point to the door.
  Clap your hands together.
  One, two, three.
  Now sit down and look at me.

Brian with five to six year olds.

2 G

Rearranging the class

TEACHER: OK, I'll show you ... but first
  of all, ... what do we do when we're
  learning a new song?
  Right. Everyone come out here ...
  to the front of the class. Uh uh ...
  Now let's start with the first row.
  You go over there and leave
  a space.
  Now the next row. And now this
  one. OK.

Cristina with seven to eight year olds.

Listen to the teacher in **2E** using a fast TPR routine. The children have been drawing and the movements are a short physical break from a longer activity.

Now listen to the teacher in **2F** saying a pointing rhyme. The rhyme ends with a line that settles the children down again quietly. The teacher is using actions and gestures that the children can follow.

Choose one of these routines to learn by heart. Practise on your own or practise doing it with a partner.

RECORD   After you have practised, record yourself saying it fast.

TPR for arranging the class

Using TPR activities from the very beginning gets children used to directions in English.

Listen to Cristina in **2G** who is going to introduce a new song. As always when teaching a new song, she wants everyone to sit on the floor close to the blackboard.

a Listen to Cristina in **2G** again and put a **/** mark between the **chunks**.

Then, in each chunk, mark the words she **stresses**. You should find one or two in each chunk.

Finally listen, pause, and repeat, trying to imitate her **intonation** and **stress** patterns.

RECORD   Then record yourself taking the teacher's part.

LANGUAGE FOCUS 2.3

Recalling routines: what do we do when ...

Cristina says:
  First of all, what do we do when we're learning a new song?
  Right, everyone come out here ....

In this case, Cristina answers her own question, but later when the children have learnt how to express this routine, they will be able to answer themselves.

  What routines do you have (or would you like to have) with your classes?
  If you have the opportunity, compare with other teachers and ask them what routines they have.

Add more ideas in the table on the next page. Adapt the instructions to suit your lessons.

RECORD Choose four or five to record on your cassette.

What do we do	when we are learning a new song?	everybody stand up
	when we are having a story?	come up and sit on the mat
	when we're reading a big book?	come and stand round the board
	when we're going to play 'follow the leader'?	everyone come out here to the front
	after cutting out and sticking?	clear everything up nicely
	at the end of the lesson?	line up – one behind the other
		get our/your bags
		line up in rows beside our/your tables
		push the front desks/tables back
		line up quietly by the door
		_____
		_____

TEACHING TIPS

Total Physical Response

✔ The first time you use TPR you can explain in the mother tongue before you start. Do simple actions and say what you are doing.

TPR with big classes

✔ If you have a large class, divide it up into groups depending on the space you have: *Six pupils go first, then six more.*
The group(s) waiting will be watching the activity, listening, and trying to understand, so will still be learning.

TOPIC TALK
Sports and hobbies

1 Here are some questions you could ask your pupils. Can you think of two or three more?
— Who likes collecting things? Who collects stamps? postcards?
— What do you collect? Do you collect badges?
— Who likes playing football? What other games do you play? Skipping? Hide and seek? Who likes swimming?
— What other hobbies do you have?
Practise asking these prompt questions and answering them as if you were a child in school.

RECORD Record yourself asking and answering the questions.

2 Do you have a favourite sport or hobby?

RECORD Prepare what you could say about it in just one minute. Record your talk.

2.4 Listening and performing – miming

Revising and consolidating topic words through mime

When children are familiar with the vocabulary used for a particular topic, you can introduce mime.

Miming means acting silently, without speaking.

The children
— have to listen carefully when you describe what they have to mime
— have to decide how to perform what you describe
— may need some thinking time for this
— move and act but do not have to speak.
Miming is more complex than simple TPR activities. TPR involves children doing everything you say. Mime gives the children more freedom to be creative.

Children have to be familiar with the language of the topic you are going to describe. Mime is very suitable for stories: as you read, ask the children to mime the key actions.

Now listen to Lucy, the teacher in **2H**. She is calling out actions to her class. This is a very simple way to mime. The children can listen and watch other children or the teacher if they have forgotten what the instructions mean. This teacher waits for the children to mime the actions – then she does the action as well.

In **2H** the whole class is miming the actions. You can also let individuals/pairs/groups mime and let the rest of the class guess what they are doing.

If children want to check meaning – they may ask you in your mother tongue. You can confirm or correct in your mother tongue, then repeat what you said in English.

2H

Miming a morning routine

TEACHER: You're washing your hands … washing your hands. Very good, washing your hands. Now you're combing your hair … combing your hair. Good, combing your hair. Now, again, wash your hands … good. Now combing your hair. Very good. Now washing your face … ah … your face, not your hands!

Lucy with seven to eight year olds.

TEACHING TIPS

Miming

✔ Give very young learners one instruction at a time.
✔ With VYLs you can say *pretend you are a squirrel.*
✔ Increase the number of instructions in a sequence as learners progress.
✔ Make the activities simpler or more complicated.
✔ Using real things can make the mime more realistic. Let children use things they make or bring in.

✔ Play a game like *statues*. The children mime an activity to music – and then stand still like statues when the music stops. Anyone who moves after the music stops is out.
✔ Later, use mime as a speaking activity and let the children describe what is happening.
✔ Groups or individual children can mime different people or animals. The others guess what or who they are miming.

Miming to rhymes and chants

All children love nursery rhymes and **chants**. Before children begin to say the words in rhymes and chants, they should understand **roughly** what they mean.
— Listening and miming helps children understand when they are learning rhymes and chants.

2I

Physical break chant

TEACHER: OK, let's have a break and do a
physical break chant. OK, so yeah it'll
be fun. So are you all ready? OK,
everyone stand. Right, now, yeah
everyone ready? OK, here we go.
    You're a tree, grow tall.
    You're a very bouncy ball.
    You're a lady, in the rain.
    You're a bird, you're a plane.
    You're a lion, you're a frog.
    You're a monkey, you're a log.

Brian with six to seven year olds.
(Based on a chant in *JET 90* – Ronald
Woods and Bill Bowler)

Listen to the teacher in **2I** using a chant to let the children do some
actions and work off some of their energy. It is called a physical break
chant and the teacher has put pictures of the items named in the chant
on the board.

TEACHING TIPS

Physical break chants

✔ Use pictures to help the children
remember the meaning of the
words.

✔ Use movements to help them
understand.

✔ Use big gestures to help them enjoy
the chant.

✔ Later once they understand some
of the words, you can gradually
remove the pictures.

You can change the chant by
✔ putting in different animals or
things you want the children
to mime

✔ making it shorter or longer

✔ letting individual children do
the actions.

Later on the children can say and do the
action rhymes on their own.

LANGUAGE FOCUS 2.4

Turn-giving

↻ Read these phrases out loud. Decide whether you want the whole class,
half the class, or smaller groups or individuals.

a Put them in order from large group to individual responses. Then say them
out loud again, if possible from memory.

RECORD Choose five to record.

1 *Everybody – all of you! Ready?*
2 *Just this row.*
3 *Maria, your turn.*
4 *OK, this group now …*
5 *Anybody else? Hands up …
one at a time … don't just
shout out.*
6 *Blue team – you start. Then red,
then yellow.*

7 *OK, yellow, your turn next.*
8 *Right, now boys and girls …
all together.*
9 *Class – you're in two halves …
OK, this half first.*
10 *Back row, then front row.*
11 *Second row, then third row.*
12 *OK, you two, then you two, next.*

2.5 Listening and responding games

You can extend the listening activities you do in class in many ways. One way is by playing games that demand careful listening.

These games help children have fun and make them listen while you are speaking English.

Right or wrong

Here is a simple response activity. You can also say *true or false?* or *true or not true?*

— Ask children to listen carefully.
— Explain that you are going to tell them something. It might be right or wrong.
— If you are wrong, they must clap twice and if you are right, they clap once.

🎧 Now listen to the teacher in 2J.

2 J

Right or wrong

TEACHER: OK, am I right or am I wrong? Listen and remember. Two claps wrong … one clap right. Now listen carefully. I know I'm right.
 OK. Today's Monday. Am I right?
(*one clap*)

TEACHER: It's sunny today.
(*two claps*)

TEACHER: Very good it's not sunny … it's raining. OK.

TEACHER: This is Anna.
(*one clap*)

TEACHER: This is Lea.
(*two claps*)

TEACHER: Oh, oh, silly me … this is Maria.

Lucy with seven to eight year olds.

LANGUAGE FOCUS 2.5

Instructions for true/false activities

Which instructions would suit your class best? Choose the best ones and record them.

If it is true	clap once, like this.
If I'm right	nod your head, like this … shout out 'yes'. put one hand up.
If it is not true	clap twice – two claps.
If I'm not right	shake your head, like this.
If I'm wrong	shout out 'no'. put both hands up, two hands up.

Simon says

This is a very popular action game. It is very easy and the children have to listen carefully, to find out whether to respond or keep still. You can play it inside or outside.

When you play 'Simon says'

— if possible, have a space where all the pupils can stand up
— with big classes choose actions that children can do sitting down
— stand in front of your pupils
— explain before you begin
— tell them they can only move when you say 'Simon says'
— explain that if you don't say 'Simon says', they must keep still
— tell them if they move when you do not say 'Simon says' – they are out
— tell them that, when they are out, they have to sit and wait for the next game.

2 K

'Simon says'

TEACHER: Put up your hands
(*No one moves.*)
TEACHER: Simon says … put up
your hands.
(*Children put hands up*)
TEACHER: Very good.
TEACHER: Simon says … put your
hands on your heads.

Brian with eight to nine year olds.

🎧 Listen to Brian in **2K** playing 'Simon says' with very simple actions.

You can use other words instead of 'Simon says'. You could use
— 'Teacher says'
— a pupil's name – 'Anna says'
— or other words such as *Please*.

🎧 Now listen to Brian, the teacher in **2L**. He is using the word *please*. When the children hear *please* they have to do the actions. When the teacher doesn't say *please*, they must stay still.

2 L

Actions please!

TEACHER: Now stand in two lines.
OK … now sh … quiet … sh …
sh … sh.
OK, quiet. Right, good. Now OK,
listen very carefully. When I say
'please' – you can move. If I don't say
'please', don't move. OK. Now let's
see who's listening.
TEACHER: One step forward.
(*No one moves!*)
TEACHER: One step back please!
(*Everyone takes a step.*)
TEACHER: Very good. You're all listening.
TEACHER: Two steps forward please.
(*Everyone takes two steps.*)
TEACHER: Turn around.
(*Some children turn.*)
TEACHER: Oh, oh! You did it and I didn't
say please! OK, you come out and
wait beside me. OK.
TEACHER: Now, jump up.
(*No one moves.*)
TEACHER: Jump up please!

Brian with eight to nine year olds.

TEACHING TIPS

Listening and responding

✔ Explain in mother tongue before you start a new game and then explain again in English.

✔ When children get good at this, make the instructions more complicated by asking the children to do two things at a time, e.g. *Stand up and comb your hair.*
✔ Later on the children can give the instructions in the action games.

REMEMBER
'Listening and doing' activities need action as a response. This lets you check immediately and you know instantly if the children understand or if they don't.

TOPIC TALK
Clothes

↻ 1 Find four or five colour pictures showing small groups of people: some children, and some adults, wearing different kinds of clothes.
Practise describing out loud in English what each person is wearing.

RECORD Choose three different people and record yourself talking about what they are each wearing.
Play back your recording (without saying which person or picture it is). Show the children all the pictures and see if they can discover which person it is you are describing.

2 How would you describe the clothes your pupils wear to school if you were talking to someone from another country?
If children are emailing penpals overseas, this is the kind of thing they can write about.

3 What clothes do people wear for different sports or jobs?

↻ Make a list of three or four kinds of clothes. Then make a quiz for someone else, for example: *The person I am thinking about is wearing a blue uniform with a blue cap.*
This person is wearing shorts, boots, and a coloured T-shirt. What do you think he is doing?

Further ideas

1 Write in your notebook
— two or three things you feel you have learnt from this unit
— two or three areas you feel you need more practice in.

2 Read the classroom extracts again.
— Choose three and mark the key words that should be **stressed**.
— Mark where the pauses might come.
🎧 — Read them out loud, trying out various intonation patterns, then listen to them on the CD, and compare your intonation and pronunciation.

3 Find a coursebook or a resource book with 'listen and do' activities such as:
Reilly, Vanessa and Sheila M. Ward. 1997. *Very Young Learners*. Oxford: Oxford University Press.
Read the Introduction and look at the activities.
— Choose two/three activities that you might do in one of your classes.
— Work out how you can introduce and set up these activities in English.
— Look through this unit to find phrases that might have been useful.
— Teach these activities, using as much English as possible.
— Write down your reactions in your notebook.

4 Teach the same activities in another class but this time take in a cassette recorder with a microphone.

RECORD Record yourself setting up and leading the 'listen and do' activities.
— Listen to your recording two or three times.
— Write down what you notice about the things you said and did.

3

This unit looks at

how listening to English and making things

- can be done without expecting children to speak English at first
- is an ideal way for children to **absorb** more English
- includes a range of activities that are suited to all levels
- helps interaction in English between teacher and pupils
- allows children to create things they can be proud of
- can include a focus on cultural **awareness**.

Listen and make

Introduction

In Unit 2 we looked at 'listening and doing', where children listen and do actions as you tell them and show them. 'Listening and making' involves children in a more creative process.

— The children have to make decisions.
— There is more time to think and comment.
— There are opportunities for **co-operation** between learners.
— The children have something to take home at the end of the class.

How to prepare for 'Listen and make' activities

When children are making things, the language that you use is the reason for the lesson. So, before the lesson,

— prepare what to tell the class about the topic or theme
— collect the things you need so you can show children what to do
— practise explaining in English what they have to make and how they have to make it
— think of **gestures** and actions that will help them understand more clearly
— prepare and practise phrases that will be useful while they are making it
— think of things children might say to you in their mother tongue and plan how you will **recast** their questions and comments in English.

How to set up 'Listen and make' activities

— Begin by introducing the topic and talking a little about it.
— Explain to the class in English (as far as possible) and show them what they are going to do or make. Use gestures and actions to help children understand.
— Repeat your instructions to the whole class and then later to small groups or to individual children.
— While they are colouring or making their things, go round and comment in English on what they are doing.

The activities in this unit go from simple colouring to more complex and more creative activities.

3.1 Listen and colour

Colouring is a very simple activity for language work with VYLs and YLs. Before you begin, make sure that all children have colours, crayons, markers, coloured pencils, or felt tipped pens.

Then prepare your learners for the activity by doing some 'Listen and identify' activities (see page oo) in order to:

— **revise** the colours they will need
— revise the names of what they are about to colour.

Give out a picture to each child. They have to listen to your instructions. You are going to tell them what colours to use and what to colour.

3 A

Listen and colour

TEACHER: Now look at this picture. OK. It's a clown. OK, I'll give you a picture.
Here you are. Ann and Patricia you can help me … a picture for Lucy. Give it to Lucy … a picture for Sam … give it to Sam …
OK, now look at your picture and point to the nose. Where's his nose?
Yes there it is. His nose.
Now, colour the nose black.
(*Children are talking in their mother tongue while they are colouring.*)

TEACHER: OK, everyone. Colour the nose black. Very good. That's really nice. Good.

TEACHER: Now show me the eyes, the clown's eyes. Yes here they are.
Now colour the eyes blue. Great.

TEACHER: Now when you've finished put up your hands. Are you finished? Very good. OK. Everyone has to colour their own picture. OK, Ann, I'll look at it later.
OK, now colour the hands. OK, please sit down Andy, OK. Thanks. Now, good.
(*after a while*)

TEACHER: OK, let's check now. Show me … point to …
Black nose, blue eyes, orange mouth, brown hair, yellow hands.
Very good. Now we'll put up the pictures on the wall today.
Very good, they're lovely.
Now let's count. OK, let's see how many clowns we have. One, two, three, four …

Brian with seven to eight year olds.

Listen to the teacher in **3A**. His class topic is the circus. The class are going to colour a picture of a clown, starting with his face.

As you listen, notice how many times the teacher
a repeats what he says
b **rephrases** things
Write down the **phrases** he uses to
c check understanding of the names for parts of the face (3 phrases)
d tell the children what colour to use (2)
e praise their efforts
f **discipline** a child who is trying to colour another child's picture and a child who is looking for attention.

TEACHING TIPS

Listen and colour

✔ Let the children help you organize and give out the materials for colouring.
✔ **Display** all the children's work – on a wall chart or on the walls.
✔ Comment positively on each child's work as you take it and put it up on the wall, e.g. *That's lovely! I like his black nose!*
✔ Use plain flashcards for colouring – children can use this set of cards later for word games.
✔ Use drawings of animals, food, clothes which can later be cut out.

✔ Make the activity more challenging:
— give out two pictures, one of a girl and one of a boy, and give two instructions at a time, e.g. *Colour his hair brown and her hair black*, etc.
— give children **alternatives**, e.g. *Colour his hair either red or yellow.*
— divide the class in two and give different instructions to each group. Later use these pairs of different pictures for games like 'Spot the difference' (see Unit 5, page 62).

LANGUAGE FOCUS 3.1

Explaining and demonstrating

Read the suggestions in the table. Change some to suit your lessons better. Add some more ideas. Practise saying them out loud or to someone else.

RECORD　Choose five to record.

Today we are going to	do some colouring. do some drawing. do some painting. do some sticking.	Look, like this … Look at what we are going to make. _____
Next, we are going to	make a monster. _____	Here's one Class 3 made. Look, here's a picture for you to colour.
Over the next few lessons we are going to	make an Easter Card. colour some animals. make a farm. make a circus picture.	Here's a sticker sheet for you to share – one between two. We'll start like this … You can all choose a different animal. _____ _____
Let's do some together as a class first, so you'll see		what I mean. what it might be like. what to do. how to do it. _____

Asking for helpers and giving things out

↻　Practise saying these phrases. If you can, act them out with a partner.

RECORD　Choose four to record.

I need two helpers, please.	So, can you give out these pictures? One each.
Who'd like to help? You three? Fine.	Can you pass round these sheets of paper? so everyone has one?
Sachiko, can you help me?	Can you give out the cards? Three for each table.
Ann and Pat – you can help me.	Hand these back down your rows. Can you find the boxes of crayons and give them out? Can you collect in the cards? Thanks.

TOPIC TALK
The circus

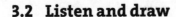

↻ **1** Look at the picture on page 33 of the clown in the circus. How many questions can you make about it? For example,
Who can see a white horse galloping round the circus ring?

↻ **2** Find a simple picture of a circus or a clown in a book.
Describe the picture in English to someone else. Ask them to draw it, listening to your description. Watch them draw. Help if they don't understand.

RECORD Describe the picture again and this time record your description on your cassette. Play it back and listen carefully.

↻ **3** Plan three or four things to say about circuses that might interest your young learners. If you are working with other people tell each other what you thought of saying.

3.2 Listen and draw

Children can draw by themselves without instructions. But your aim is to get them to listen to some instructions in English.
As in Topic Talk above, you can describe a very simple picture of a familiar scene, with objects children know. The children listen and draw what they hear you describe.

🎧 Listen to **3B** but do not read the extract as you listen. The children are going to draw a picture. They have already drawn a large square on a piece of paper, to act as a frame for their picture. Draw an empty frame for yourself. As you listen, try to draw what the teacher says. Then listen again and read the text to check what you have drawn.

🎧 Now listen again to **3B**. Pay attention to the **intonation** the teacher uses.

RECORD Record yourself taking the teacher's part.

Extension ideas

Choose three or four pictures the children have drawn and show them to the class.
— Talk about things in them to the whole class.
— Put two up on the board and talk about the differences or ask the children to spot the difference:
How many differences can you find?
— Make up a story about what is happening or talk about what might happen later:
The cat might eat the birds.

3 B

Listen and draw

TEACHER: So, are you ready to draw? OK, so ... sh. OK, so listen, listen. On the left, this side, the left side, draw a tree, a big tree ... OK, like so, a very big tree! On the left ... OK. Wow – that's a big tree, Mei Li. Great. Fantastic! ... So you've all got a tree in your picture? OK. Shall I go on?

SOME CHILDREN: Yes.

TEACHER: OK, at the top of the tree, draw two small birds ... OK, two little birds. OK, so they are sitting near the top of the tree. OK, two little birds ... Uh uh. Good. Good.

TEACHER: And under the tree, on the right, but very near the tree, is a cat ... OK, a cat ... Ah Hong, what's the matter? Nothing? OK ... That's good. So, a cat under the tree, on the right and ...

What do you think the cat wants to do? OK. Can he see the birds? Maybe he's very hungry ... (*Children are chatting in their mother tongue and some are making cat sounds miaou.*)

TEACHER: Right, OK, so you've all got a tree, two birds, and a cat in your picture? That's it, good ... OK, now ...

On the right ... on the right of the picture, draw a bus stop. OK, not a bus, just a bus stop. That's right, Chiu Ming. Look, a bus stop. OK, everybody got a bus stop now? Yes? OK, OK ... So, now draw yourself. OK, draw you, somewhere in the picture. Anywhere. OK. You could be ... eh ... like by the bus stop. OK. You could be near the cat. Stroking the cat, like this ... Yea. Or you could be in the tree. It's up to you. You decide. You decide where you are ... OK.

(*Later on when the pupils are finishing their drawing.*)

And finally, finally a snake. Anywhere you like. OK, a snake ... Yea, right.

(*The children react to the idea of a snake – with mother-tongue comments.*)

And now, I want you to write your name in the corner of your picture for me. Here, in the corner. Good. Well done everybody.

(*Drawing continues*)

Brian with nine to ten year olds.

TEACHING TIPS

Listen and draw

✔ After drawing let children compare pictures and then colour them quietly.

✔ Go round and talk to them in English as they colour, and comment on their work like this teacher:

Ah, Mei Li, so you have coloured your birds red and green, like parrots. Very pretty ... Mmmm. That's a nice green tree, Eng Soon ... but where's your cat? Oh, I see him, hiding behind the tree.

LANGUAGE FOCUS 3.2a

Phrases describing position

Here are some phrases that are useful for describing pictures.

1   **a**   Find seven pairs of phrases that are opposite in meaning.
      b   Which two phrases are left over?

1	on the left	a	in the background, far away
2	in the middle – a bit to the left	b	under the tree
3	in the corner, at the front	c	at the front
4	at the top of the tree	d	in the corner, at the back
5	at the back	e	in front of the tree
6	next to the tree	f	on the right
7	right at the front of the picture	g	in the middle – a bit to the right
8	behind the tree	h	by the bus stop

Can you put several phrases together to make a very long one? Add any other words you like, for example:

In the corner, at the top, on the left just behind the top of the tree.

↻ Practise saying the long phrases fast on your own or to a partner. Give your partner the picture you drew when listening to the CD. Ask them to draw a tiny cross in the place you describe.

RECORD   Then record three long phrases on your cassette.

Drawing games

A drawing game helps everyone to work together and the children have to listen. Explain everything clearly at the beginning.

🎧 Listen to Juan in **3C**. He is beginning a game called 'Draw the monster'. He has already prepared his class for this game. He has checked to see if the children remember the parts of the body he is going to use in the game. Later he checks these words again to make sure the children remember them. Finally he sticks the picture cards on the board in this order:

a nose – a body – a head – an eye – a foot – an arm – a hand – an ear – a leg – a mouth

3 C

Monster drawing game

TEACHER: OK, everyone's ready … well, almost. Now, let's see. Here are the pictures on the board. OK, in a line like this, we have a nose, a body, a head, an eye, a foot, an arm, a hand, an ear, a leg, a mouth. And you are in three teams, team A, team B, team C. And we will all count. OK?

OK, OK. This group is the first group. So let's begin. Take out the dice. OK, Laura you throw the dice for your team.

Right, five. OK, let's count together. One, two, three, four, five, OK. Five is foot. So everyone draw a foot. OK, just draw a foot. OK …

OK, this team now. OK, so throw the dice OK … four … OK, continue. One, two, three, four … a leg.

OK, it's a leg. So, now you draw a leg. Right.

So now we've got a foot and a leg. OK, is there a mistake? Now only one foot and only one leg – fantastic!

OK. Good David. Only one leg and one foot.

OK, this team, team A! Take the dice and throw it. Not at me! Come on!

OK, what have you got?

Juan with eight to nine year olds.

LANGUAGE FOCUS 3.2b

Useful phrases

⟳ Read through the class extracts you listened to in **3.1** and **3.2**. Write down any useful phrases you find. Underline the **key words** – the words you would **stress** – and say the whole phrase out loud.

🎧 Listen again to these extracts on the CD and pause and repeat each phrase a few times.

RECORD Finally, choose some phrases to record on to your own cassette.

Asking who wants a turn

2 In 3C the teams took turns to throw the dice.
In **2.4** we looked at expressions for turn-giving – *OK, Paula, you start.*
But sometimes you can ask who wants a turn.

⊶ Read out the phrases below, then choose four, and think of what you could say to a learner who responds, for example, *Whose turn is it to do a mime? OK, Mei Li, so you want to show us your mime? Out you come, then.*

— Who wants to start? Hands up!
— Whose go is it?
— Whose turn is it to do a mime?
— One more go. Who wants the last go?
— Blue team? But you started last time.

— Maria again? But you've just had a go.
— Who has still not had a turn?
— Who still wants a go?
— Which group has not been?

Extension ideas

— Make a wall chart of a monster house and let the children put their monsters in different rooms.
— Get the children to draw or stick in cut out furniture. Use other fun topics for drawing, such as witches, ghosts, or clowns.

✔ After drawing monsters ask children to colour them.
✔ Hold up a picture and describe the monster to the class. You could make this into a *Right or wrong* game – see 2.5, page 29.

3D

Making a card

TEACHER: Now, look at what we are going to make. We're going to make a Mother's Day card.
(*The children are moving around.*)

TEACHER: Alright, we're going to make it. We're going to do it this way.
Now look, take the piece of paper, see the line, cut, fold, colour, write your name. Are you ready? Play a game.
(*The teacher uses gestures to explain the words cut, fold, colour, write your name.*)

TEACHER: OK, everybody. Listen again, cut, fold, colour, write your name.
Are you ready? Play a game.
Now, OK, now, come here, now Ann and Peter give these out. This is the paper you are going to use. OK, OK…
Let me see everyone sitting down…
OK, let me see everyone sitting down.
Alright, now, the scissors. One pair between two desks is enough.
OK, I'll go around and look.
Yes, OK, Lara, yes. Yes Tom, yes. Look … cut like this. Only cut that bit.
No Pat. OK, I'll show you. OK, fold it like that …

Jane with seven to eight year olds.

3.3 Listen and make

There are many things that children can make in class, for example, they can make models out of modelling clay, **plasticine**, **play-dough**, paper, or card. They can make posters to go on a wall. And it is always fun making things for a special occasion. Children love celebrations and festivals.

➲ Think of all the occasions you can celebrate with children. Make a list of some things your pupils could bring in to school to show you on some of these occasions.
— Personal events, e.g. birthdays, coming back to school after a holiday …
— Festivals and special days
    — in your country
    — in other countries
    — in English-speaking countries.
Use opportunities such as these to talk in English about the things children bring in. Tell the children what happens during celebrations in other countries. Some of the days may be celebrated in your country, as well, but in a different way.

Making greeting cards

In English-speaking countries people send cards on special days such as Christmas, Valentine's Day, Mother's Day, Father's Day, Easter, and on someone's birthday.

➲ Think of what materials you would need to make a Mother's Day card, and how you would tell your learners how to make it. Write down some things you might say.

🎧 Listen to the teacher in **3D** telling her class of eight year olds what to do. Notice how she
— tells the children what to do and shows them with gestures
— gives them worksheets with drawings
— asks the children to share the scissors between pairs
— tells all the children together
— walks around and helps each child.

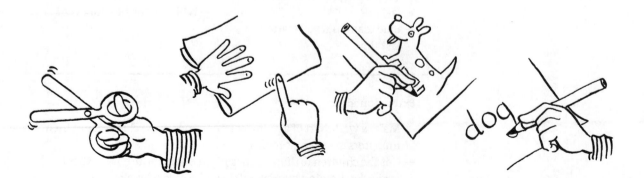

LANGUAGE FOCUS 3.3a

Language for demonstration

a The teacher in **3D** uses a lot of language for demonstration. Read these phrases out loud. Which phrase is the odd one out? Can you explain why?

We're going to do it this way …   *Look, cut like this. Only cut that bit …*
Now look … see the line …   *No Pat. OK, I'll show you …*
One between two desks …   *OK, fold it like that …*

Making an Easter card

Now listen to the teacher in **3E**. She is preparing her class to make an Easter card – she is reminding the children of what she told them about Easter and giving them more information. The teacher
— talks about Easter
— talks about what they already know about – the Easter Bunny (see page 12)
— prepares for the 'listen and make' part of the lesson
— shows the children how to cut out the Easter Bunny
— uses words to show where to cut – as she cuts
— repeats to children in groups or individually
— praises their work.

3 E

Cutting out and sticking

TEACHER: Lots of lovely Easter Bunnies.
Now watch me first. I take my scissors and cut. Let's see … I'll start with the bunny's head. OK, I have to be careful. Cut round the head and now his big ears … his big ears that go flop, flop, flop. And up the ear and down again and round his head. Now, here round the bunny's face and round his shoulder and down round his body and now down to his feet, that go …

What do his feet do? They go hop, hop, hop.

OK, round this side and back to his head. Now I'm going to stick my bunny on the card. I'll put the glue on the back and stick it now. I'll put my card here on the board.

OK. Now, you take your scissors and you can start and I'll go around and look at you cutting. Now be careful. Go slowly.

OK, John. You're starting at his head. Very good. Now you're going round his head. Very good. And his ears. Good

OK, Lea, let me see. Yes that's good. Do you want me to help? OK …

Cathy with eight to nine year olds.

LANGUAGE FOCUS 3.3b

Cutting things out

b How many phrases can you find in this transcript with the words:
round   up   down   back   on

e.g. *Cut round the head.*

Practise saying them very slowly and clearly, as if to a class who are cutting things out.

Listen to the CD again.

RECORD   Choose five phrases to record.

What do you keep where?

⤴ Read the lists below. Add to the lists of things, containers, and places.

Pencils, crayons, felt-tipped pens, markers, rulers, paints, paint brushes, scissors, glue, plasticine, play-dough, paper, coloured paper, large sheets of paper, card, cleaning cloths, sponges, paper towels...

in boxes,   in packets,
in jars,   in envelopes,
in plastic tubs,   in folders ...

on the shelf,   on top of the cupboard,
on the top/bottom/   in the painting corner,
middle shelf,   in the book corner,
in the cupboard,   near the rubbish bin/trashcan,
       on the tray in the corner...

⤴ Now practise six requests, asking your children to get things out or put them away, using patterns like these:

Can you get the _____ out? Do you know where it is/they are?
Can you put the _____ away? Do you know where it goes/they go?
Yes, on the ...

RECORD   Record them on your own cassette.

🎧 Pronunciation point

⊶ **Sounds /θ/ and /ð/**

⤴ **1** These ten words all have *th* in their spelling. Say them out loud.

thanks	*there*	*the*	*mother*	*three*
this	*that*	*throw*	*thin*	*they*

How would you sort them into two groups?

RECORD **2** Either record yourself or work with a partner and say these pairs of words in any order:

three ... three   *three ... tree*
tree ... tree   *tree ... three*

Play back your recording or get someone to listen to you and decide if the pairs you have said are the same or different.

TEACHING TIPS

Making things

✔ Let children
— become familiar with all the names they need for drawing and painting:
  crayons, scissors, brushes
— take charge of materials such as the paper, the colours, the scissors.
— find materials in the places where you keep them:
  on top of cupboard ... in the painting corner.

✔ Talk to small groups/individuals while they work.
✔ Cut out shapes of all the name sets children are working with – such as animals, monsters, food and drinks, etc. Keep them in envelopes. You can use them for guessing games or for 'mix and match' games or to put **labels** on.

TOPIC TALK
Festivals and celebrations

1 Prepare to talk to your classes about a local festival that your children know about.

o– Write down questions you might ask the children.

2 Find out about one or two of these festivals and special days:
Chinese New Year, Divali/Deepavali (Hindu), Christmas (Christian), Yom Kippur (Jewish), Eid el Fitr – end of Ramadan (Muslim), Mother's Day, Father's Day … and prepare to tell your pupils what happens.
Look for pictures of festivals in books, and plan how you would talk about them.

RECORD If possible plan a short talk about a festival (two minutes maximum), and find some pictures to illustrate your talk. Present it to your colleagues and record it (at the same time) on your cassette.

Further ideas

1 Plan how you would get your children working in groups to make a poster about one particular festival. Plan a series of lessons. Work out what stages you could do in each lesson. Plan how you would explain everything, at each stage.
Write out this plan. Add in samples of language you could use at each stage.

2 Listen again to all the useful phrases you recorded while doing this unit. Practise again the ones you will find most useful.

3 Find a coursebook or resource book with some 'listen and make' activities such as Reilly, Vanessa and Sheila M. Ward. 1997. *Very Young Learners*. Oxford: Oxford University Press.

Read the Introduction of the book you found, and
— choose a 'listen and make' activity that you might try in one of your classes
— work out how you can introduce and set it up in English
— plan what you will say at each stage
— teach the activity, using as much English as possible
— write down your reactions in your notebook.

4 Look back through this unit to find phrases that might have been useful; teach the same activity again but this time take in a cassette recorder with a microphone:
RECORD — record yourself
— listen to your recording and write down what you have learnt from doing this.

4

This unit looks at

how to encourage children in their first efforts to speak English by

- encouraging the use of set classroom phrases
- introducing new vocabulary using pictures, gestures, and repetition
- helping learners remember new words and phrases in **context**
- teaching pronunciation and vocabulary together
- collecting suitable rhymes and songs.

Speaking with support

Introduction

In the last two units we looked at how to increase children's listening time. The more children listen, the better. When they are listening they
— are still actively learning
— are **acquiring** language and learning to understand
— are **absorbing** pronunciation and intonation
— can repeat what they hear
— can answer or comment in their mother tongue.

In this unit, the focus is on pupils' responding and beginning to speak some English. All the listening activities we looked at in Units 2 and 3 could lead on to speaking activities.

You can support children when they are starting to speak English
— by using English in the way we described in Unit 1 as **caretaker talk**
— by encouraging all the efforts children make to speak English, no matter how small
— by listening carefully when they speak and not interrupting to correct small errors.

4.1 Using classroom phrases

Pupils respond to their teacher (see **2.1**).
They
— ask you questions and tell you things they want you to know
— often repeat comments and requests
— can easily learn to repeat the **set expressions** you use during their English lesson.

Read what the children in the drawing are saying. There are three empty speech bubbles. What are they going to say?

Think of what your pupils say to you in their mother tongue in class. Think of what they
— ask you
— tell you.

Make a list of what you could help them to say in English.

When children repeat set phrases it does not necessarily mean language **acquisition** is taking place.

But they are
— getting used to saying English sounds
— practising the intonation pattern
— gaining confidence, especially if you praise them or show your approval in other ways.

> **REMEMBER**
> — When children are learning their first language they hear phrases and understand the general meaning before they understand individual words.
> — They hear connected sounds before they separate them into individual words.
> — Only written language is divided into words and sentences.
> — Young learners who cannot read hear a flow of sound.
> — They hear intonation patterns, and sounds or words that are stressed. These are the sounds they will say first.

It is best to introduce useful classroom phrases in the situation in which they are normally used.

Listen to the teacher in **4A** introducing a phrase during a game. His pupils are playing 'clothes dominoes' with cards. The cards show coloured clothes. The children play in turns by putting down the same colour or the same clothes item beside the domino card that is on the table. They are all playing in small groups and the teacher is working with one group.

The phrase they learn can be used again whenever they are playing games or taking turns.

4 A

Learning a new phrase in context

TEACHER: OK, Midori, red shoes …
MIDORI: Red jumper.
HARUKA: A purple skirt.
TEACHER: Can't you go?
HARUKA: No.
TEACHER: OK, I can't go, say 'I can't go'.
HARUKA: I can't go.
TEACHER: Good, OK, now the next card. How do you say this in English? trou … trou
PUPILS AND TEACHER: Trousers.
TEACHER: Good. OK, your turn now.
HARUKA: Blue trousers.
TEACHER: Good.
MIDORI: I can't go.
TEACHER: No – you haven't got anything blue.
MIDORI: No – I can't go.
TEACHER: OK.

Bob with eleven to twelve year olds.

LANGUAGE FOCUS 4.1

What learners need to say and ask

a In the first two boxes below there are some possible things children might need to tell you. Add more things to the children's boxes. Then select a suitable response from the teacher in the second box.

RECORD   Practise and then record three possible conversations.

Children	
I haven't got	my pencils.
I've lost	my colours.
I've forgotten	my book.
Look, I've got	a new bag/pencil case.
	some new felt tipped pens.

Teacher	
Has anyone seen Giorgio's pencil/book/colours?	Did you leave it at home? OK, never mind.
Can someone lend Giorgio a pencil/some colours?	Here's one. Here you are.
	Go and get one from my table.
Who's got a spare pencil?	Leila – can he look at your book?
Don't worry – I've got a spare one/set here.	Can he share with you?
	That's/Those are lovely. Who gave you that/those?

RECORD   Add to the table below and practise some possible exchanges. Then record three on your cassette.

Child	Teacher
Excuse me! Can you help me?	Yes – of course, just coming.
Please Miss X! Is this right?	Wait a moment, Ana, I'm just helping Peter. Yes … what is it you need?
I don't know what to do!	That's fine like that.
Please can I ask in Spanish?	Yes … What do you need to know?

4.2 Saying rhymes and singing songs to practise pronunciation, stress, and intonation

We've already looked at how children love doing actions when they watch and listen to their teacher saying rhymes and chants (see **2.4**). Children soon begin to repeat the words as they do the actions. They are speaking with the teacher. This builds confidence and a feeling of **achievement**. Children usually like singing and performing. It helps them feel at ease with English. They enjoy learning songs and rhymes they can sing or say to their parents at home.

As children acquire more English, chants, rhymes, and songs can form a real part of the learning process. Think about how you could use them in your lessons
— for enjoyment
— as part of your teaching plan
— as a change in activity
— to revise vocabulary
— to connect with new or familiar topics
— to practise up-to-date expressions
— for drama and to practise punctuation.

Think about choosing a song or rhyme. A song or rhyme should
— suit your pupils' age group and their interests
— match their level of English
— have a catchy, easy to remember melody.

Children often sing a song or say a chant or rhyme all together. However, when they are very familiar with the rhymes, songs, and chants they can perform them by singing or saying different parts in groups. This group performance is very useful with big classes. It helps develop teamwork but it still allows everyone to take part.

Read this chant about animals. The children can say it in groups as they ask and answer questions. The teacher could start by checking to see if everyone is ready:

OK, are you ready? All the groups ready? Spiders?
OK. Beetles? Puppies and sheep?
OK, now question group, you start one, two, three …

Question group	Who's having fun?
Spider group	Spiders in the sun.
Question group	Who's having lunch?
Beetle group	Beetles in a bunch.
Question group	Who's chewing socks?
Puppies group	Puppies in a box.
Question group	Who's fast asleep?
Sheep group	Three black sheep.

(Chant by Carolyn Graham)

↻ Practise reading the chant out loud in a lively way.

Songs, rhymes, and chants

✔ Start with very short rhymes or chants.
✔ Look for songs and chants that have topics your children are learning about.
✔ Make sure the children generally understand what they are saying – they do not need to understand every word but maybe the **gist** of the lines.

✔ Use songs and rhymes to play with sounds: speaking softly – shouting loudly.
✔ Use simple instruments to add to the rhythm, such as tambourine, bell, drum, cymbal.
✔ Encourage your pupils to say them for family and friends outside school.

LANGUAGE FOCUS 4.2

How loud?

Re-order these phrases in order of **volume** – from softest to loudest. Read them aloud in this new order, and then say them so that they illustrate what they mean (i.e. if it says *whisper*, then whisper it, if it says *very slowly*, then say it very slowly). Have fun trying this out. Make up one more of your own.

RECORD   Then record all five.

1   Now say it very slowly and quietly.
2   OK – everybody whisper it! Just whisper!
3   Stand well apart from each other – now each person/group can take turns to shout their part. But not too loud!
4   Normal voices – nice and clear. Not too loud, not too soft.
5   Now, can you say it fairly quietly, but very fast?

TOPIC TALK
Spiders, beetles, and small creatures

Which of these small creatures do your pupils know something about? Add others to the list.

spiders	beetles	caterpillars
butterflies	worms	snails
bees	wasps	flies

1   Write down two things that children might know or ought to know about each of these creatures:

Spiders have eight legs.
They are usually black or brown.
Spiders make webs.
They eat flies and other insects.

2   Think of two questions you might ask children about each creature:
What do bees say? Have you ever been stung by a wasp or bee?

RECORD **3** Record yourself telling someone else about four of these creatures, as if you were telling a class of young learners. Ask two questions about them and give possible answers.

4 Do you know any books or stories about any of these small creatures? Prepare to tell a colleague about one of them, *The Very Hungry Caterpillar* by Eric Carle, a well-known book for children. In this story the caterpillar ate through an apple on Monday, two pears on Tuesday, three plums on Wednesday, four strawberries on Thursday and so on, until on the Saturday he ate so much that he got tummy ache.

4.3 Practising new vocabulary

When children are listening to you they often repeat words and phrases naturally and spontaneously. When you are introducing new vocabulary and learners want to speak, you can
— encourage them to repeat the new items
— use pictures, sounds, and other senses, e.g. touch and feel materials, to support meaning
— use **gestures**, movement, and actions
— get children to colour pictures of the new things they can name
— repeat new words as often as possible and use them in **context**.
All of these methods will help your pupils become familiar with new vocabulary.

Just like children learning their first language, they can practise and play with new sounds.

Teachers have different ways of introducing and practising new words.

Listen to the teacher in **4B**. She is
— connecting new vocabulary with what her pupils already know
— using pictures to help them understand and remember
— showing her class a small part of the picture first and asking them to guess the animal (moving from a part to a whole is a good memory aid)
— teaching meaning and sound first.

> **REMEMBER**
> — If your pupils cannot read yet they have to remember the word as a sound.
> — If your pupils can read it is better if they first remember the sound of the word and then learn the spelling.

4 B

Introducing new vocabulary

TEACHER: Very good. Now, we have some new animals …
(*Teacher holds up a picture card but only shows the animal's ears.*)
TEACHER: What's this?
CHILD: It's a dog
TEACHER: A dog? No … like a dog. It's a … a fox
(*Teacher puts the picture on the board.*)
TEACHER: Now what's this?
CHILD: A fox
TEACHER: Yes, OK, one more new animal …
(*Now the teacher covers the picture with her hand so only the nose and upper face is showing.*)
TEACHER: Is this a dog?
CHILDREN: No.
TEACHER: A kangaroo?
CHILD: No.
TEACHER: An elephant?
CHILD: No.
TEACHER: No, it's a mouse … a mouse. Repeat please.
PUPILS AND TEACHER: A mouse.

Pura with nine to ten year olds.

4 C

Either/or questions

TEACHER: Now, remember, this was a?
CHILDREN: A fox.
TEACHER: And this is …?
CHILD: A mouse.
TEACHER: OK, and look at this picture. OK. Is this an elephant or a kangaroo?
CHILDREN: An elephant.
TEACHER: Yes. Good, an elephant. OK, and this one … Is this a mouse or a frog?
CHILDREN: A mouse.
TEACHER: Very good. Now …

Pura with nine to ten year olds.

4 D

Classifying

TEACHER: Now let's draw two houses. One big and one small. This is the big animal house and the other one is the small animal house. OK. Now what's this?
CHILDREN: Mouse.
TEACHER: OK, a mouse. Which house does he go in?
CHILDREN: Small house.
TEACHER: Yes. The small animal house. Very good, now, let's see …

Lucy with nine to ten year olds.

The teacher then **elicits** more animal names in **4C** by asking the children *either/or* questions.

Now listen to another class where the teacher is asking the children to **classify** animals into big and small. This is an easy way to extend any activity and it lets children
— repeat for a purpose
— practise new vocabulary
— **consolidate** vocabulary they already know.

Children are learning new things all the time so it's easy for them to forget. To help children remember it's a good idea to use new words and phrases several times in different ways. The teachers in **4B**, **4C**, and **4D** used
— guessing
— *either/or* questions
— classifying.
By doing these or similar activities you can give children extra opportunities to listen and repeat what is new and go back over what they know. In this way new and old come together in the child's memory.

Teaching new vocabulary

✔ Make class **displays** of pictures and other memory aids to support new vocabulary.
✔ Prepare to teach new words and phrases in a meaningful way by linking with a topic they are familiar with.

LANGUAGE FOCUS 4.3

Five ways of eliciting language

Play recordings **4B**, **4C**, and **4D** again, and listen to the teachers' intonation when **eliciting** a word from the children. When you **elicit** it is like asking a question. So, in the transcript, eliciting is followed by a question mark.

⊶ Here are five ways of eliciting. Can you find any more examples of these in the transcript?

a *Wh-* questions: *What's this?*
b Questions using intonation only: *A dog?*
c Questions using inversion: *Is this an elephant?*
d Unfinished sentence questions with rising intonation: *This was a … ?*
e *Either/or* questions: *Is this an elephant or a kangaroo?*

RECORD Practise these and record them on to your cassette.

🎧 Play recordings **4B**, **4C**, and **4D** again, and listen to the teachers' intonation patterns when they ask pupils to respond.

↻ RECORD Pause after each question, and repeat what the teacher says. Then select two examples of two or three different types of question to record on your cassette.

🎧 ## Pronunciation point

Two sounds

⊶ Each of these **sets** of words has a different sound in common. Say them and decide what the sounds are.

1 *phrase, four, elephant, fold, laughing*
2 *jumper, orange, jam, strange, jeans*

Can you think of any other common words with these sounds?

4.4 **Playing vocabulary games**

Guessing games and memory games are useful to help children become familiar with new vocabulary in an enjoyable way.

When you show children what to do and at the same time give instructions for games in English, they are listening to you with a real purpose – to find out how to play. They are also absorbing new vocabulary and intonation patterns.

🎧 Listen to the teacher in **4E**. She is going back over six new words. She taught them to her class earlier using pictures. The class have repeated and practised the words. Now the teacher wants to see if they can remember the words without seeing the pictures. They have to guess the picture. This is what happens.

After giving some instructions:

— The teacher takes one of the pictures.
— She doesn't let the class see it.
— She asks the children to guess what the word is.
— The child who guesses correctly comes up and takes the next picture.
— He does not show it to the other children.
— He whispers the word to the teacher.
— If he forgets the word in English, he can say it in his mother tongue and the teacher tells him the word in English and the sound.
— The others have to guess what it is.

This vocabulary game continues until all the cards have been guessed and put on the board.

4 E

Guessing the picture

TEACHER: So, let's see who remembers? I have a picture here … of something you know … Can you guess what it is?
CHILD: Star.
TEACHER: Very good. That's right. Now you come out … pick one. Do you know what it is? Whisper it to me. Yes that's it. OK, off you go …
FIRST CHILD: What is it?
SECOND CHILD: Sun.
FIRST CHILD: No.
THIRD CHILD: Garden.
FIRST CHILD: No.
FOURTH CHILD: Planet.
FIRST CHILD: No.
FIFTH CHILD: Clou.
FIRST CHILD: Yes.
TEACHER: OK, let's just check pronunciation. Is it clou or cloud?
CHILDREN: (*all together*) Cloud.
TEACHER: Cloud. Yes very good.

Jane with seven to eight year olds.

4 F

Remembering a list

TEACHER: OK, we'll start with these four. OK, are you ready?

FIRST CHILD: I'd like an apple.

SECOND CHILD: I'd like an apple and a pear.

TEACHER: Good.

THIRD CHILD: I'd like an apple and a pear – and an orange.

TEACHER: Good.

FOURTH CHILD: I'd like an orange … no … an apple and a pear and an orange and a … banana.

TEACHER: Very good. That was great, now …

Brian with nine to ten year olds.

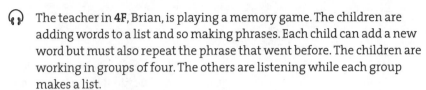 The teacher in **4F**, Brian, is playing a memory game. The children are adding words to a list and so making phrases. Each child can add a new word but must also repeat the phrase that went before. The children are working in groups of four. The others are listening while each group makes a list.

Instead of objects, you can play this game with actions, also using pictures, if necessary. For example, a possible list might be:

Mun Ling went shopping and Chui Meng went swimming and …
I went jogging.

Other games that require just a few **set expressions** plus a few other words are:

FINDING PAIRS: a memory game where children have to pick up two cards with the same picture or word. (The cards are spread out face-down.)

SHOPPING GAMES: children act the parts of shop assistants and customers in different kinds of shops to practise different vocabulary.

HAPPY FAMILIES: a card game: players in groups of three or four have to collect four cards from each other from the same 'family' or topic.

TEACHING TIPS

Vocabulary games

✔ Show children how to play the game and give instructions in English while you are doing this.

✔ Use lots of different games but use the same vocabulary to help children become familiar with it.

✔ New words and phrases need to be used a lot after you have introduced them so that the children learn to use them actively.

LANGUAGE FOCUS 4.4

Instructions for games

↻ 1 Read transcript **4E** and repeat both sets of instructions the teacher gives. Notice how she speaks in short **chunks**.

↻ 2 Read the two sample sets of instructions below: 'Find a pair' and 'Shopping game'. Think what actions you would do as you explain to your learners to help them understand.

Find a pair

Here are 12 picture cards of fruit; there are two cards with apples, two with oranges and so on. I'm going to put the cards face down on the table. You have to try to find two the same and say what they are. The person who has the most pairs at the end wins the game. Now, watch carefully and see where they all go. OK, I'm putting an apple here and an orange here … – and so on. Now they are all down. But do remember you have to say what they are before you keep the pair.

OK, one at a time. Who wants to try first? Pick one, turn it over, say what it is, then try to remember where the other one is. If you are right, you can keep the pair. If you are wrong, put them back again, face down. Look, like this …

An apple. Now I've got an apple, so I need another apple … I need another apple. Oh no ! that's a banana. OK, I'll put them back.

Now who would like to try to find a pair – two the same?

A shopping game

Let's play shopping. What kind of shop shall we have today? A pet shop?

OK. Here are the cards with pets. Who wants to be the pet shop assistant? Ah Bin? OK. Come out here. Everybody else think what you want to buy. What else could you buy in this pet shop? Could you buy any of these?

kittens   puppies   mice   hamsters
snakes   spiders   fish …

What does the customer say and what does the assistant say?

Good morning	*Good morning*
I'd like a kitten please.	*Yes, of course.*
How much?	*Ten dollars.*
Here you are.	*Thanks.*

3 Divide these instructions into short chunks/phrases. Put a dash like this – between each chunk. Then read them out loud, as if speaking to a class. Practise these instructions, adapting them if you need to, until you can say them fluently without reading.

4 Make or find a set of suitable picture cards, then record yourself giving instructions.

What can you do with cards?

a Look at the tables. Read three or four sets of instructions out loud from each table. Record them on your cassette.

RECORD

b Test yourself. Cover the tables up. Write a list of verbs/actions that you can use with cards, e.g. *mix them up*. If you can remember seven you have done very well.

Here are some cards.	Can you	give them out?	You should have three each.
These are picture cards.		deal them out?	Each pair should have six.
	Will you	share them round?	
These are word cards.			Check you have eight on each table.
Here are some cards with phrases on.		mix them up?	
		put them face down on your table?	Put the rest in a pile, face down.
Here are some cards with actions on.			

Don't look at them yet.	Don't show them to anyone else.
Just look at your own.	Don't look at anyone else's.
Spread them out so you can see them all.	Which ones make a pair?

Whoops!	One's gone in your lap.	Can you pick it up?
Oh dear!	One's fallen in your bag.	Can you reach it?
Watch out!	One's gone under your chair.	Who hasn't got all six?
Careful!	One's fallen on the floor.	Who's got one missing?
Wait a minute!	You've got an extra one.	Who's got one extra?
	You are one short.	

TEACHING TIPS

✔ When children are familiar with shopping play routines, you can have two or three shop assistants and more customers. Then they can play in groups.

✔ With more advanced learners you can add lines to the script:
Can I help you? What colour? White, please.

4.5 Practising pronunciation of new sounds

Children acquire pronunciation and intonation naturally by listening to you. When you talk they absorb the sound of the language. But this does not mean that they will produce perfect words or phrases when they begin to speak in English. They need
— to try out the sounds
— to play with sounds
— your help and praise all the time.
Young children naturally like playing with language. They can mimic new sounds more easily than older learners. When you praise their efforts you are motivating them to try again.

You can play games to encourage them to practise the sounds of English.

'I spy with my little eye' is a fun way to get children used to hearing new sounds. You can play it like this:
— Tell the children '*I spy with my little eye something beginning with 'sh'* [*or /ʃ/*].
— The children guess.
— The first child to guess correctly comes to the front.
— This child tells you a new word (in their mother tongue – or in English).
— Then you can say the first sound of the word to the child.
— The child waits while the others guess.

🎧 Listen to the teacher in **4G**, Jane, playing the game. She has pictures on the wall that the children have just used for another game. The children can see the words they are remembering.

4 G

Supporting pupils by saying a word

TEACHER: OK, we're going to play one more game…
     Do you remember… this game we played? You have to point to what I am thinking about.
     (*Teacher sits on a chair and starts game.*)

TEACHER: I spy with my little eye something beginning with 'pl'.
     (*One child points to a picture of planet on the board.*)

TEACHER: Very good Anna … pl … planet, pl … planet.
     (*Now Anna whispers her word to the teacher 'sun, sun' and she sits on chair.*)

TEACHER: Now Anna's word … I spy with my little eye … something beginning with /s/ … Can anyone point to something beginning with /s/?

Jane with seven to eight year olds.

✔ In the classroom
— you can arrange pictures of words with the same sound together:
blue – shoe – two
— if the children can read, add the written word underneath
— use actions to help children remember the face movement that produces the sound:
Stretch your arms for wide mouth sounds.

✔ Use other expressions when you are playing the game 'I spy'.
I can hear with my little ear a word beginning with …
I can remember … I can remember a word beginning with …
✔ You can use this little activity at any time and for one or two words to remind children of sounds and vocabulary.

TOPIC TALK
Animals

a Make lists of animals that children know about under four headings:

pets   farm animals
wild animals/zoo animals   nasty or scary animals

b For each animal think of two or three things to tell children about it and one or two questions to ask them. Write these down and then choose five to record. Also write down and record your responses to the answers you think they might give.

Further ideas

1 Rewind your own cassette and listen to everything you recorded while doing this unit. Practise the things you find most useful. Re-record any you would like to improve on.

2 Choose one section from this unit, and decide which activity to try out in class. Write down
— the instructions you will give in English
— the phrases you want your children to say when they are doing the activity.
Teach the activity, using as much English as possible. If possible, record the lesson.
— After the lesson, write down how it went in your notebook.
— Listen to the recording if you made one.
— Write down what you might change if you do it again.

3 Find some simple card games in a Resource Pack, or make some cards for the games in this unit. Work out two sets of instructions you could give in English to play them with very young learners and then older children.
RECORD Record at least one version of your instructions.

4 Read the Introduction to Chapter 7 from Philips, Sarah. 1993. *Young Learners*. Oxford: Oxford University Press (if you have it). Choose a song or chant that you could try in one of your classes. Write down the instructions you might give in order to set it up in English.
RECORD Then record yourself doing it with a class.

5

Speaking more freely

Introduction

In Unit 4 you saw how you can
— encourage learners to use **set expressions** for classroom routines
— introduce useful phrases in the **context** of games and activities
— stay within a familiar topic framework
— develop a topic to extend children's vocabulary
— **rephrase** and extend what children say
— accept and respect children's efforts at communicating meaning,
  even if they don't produce perfect words or phrases
— create a positive environment so that children do not feel
  embarrassed.

In this unit we are going to look at how you can help children to
continue speaking for a longer time.

5.1 Cognitive development and language learning

Children as learners

When teaching language, we also need to think of the whole child, and
encourage general **cognitive** and educational development.

This is one reason why choice of topics is important. Topics may be
familiar ones, but should be built on or extended so that learners can
learn something new. For example,

— when talking about animals, tell children one or two things they may
  not already know.
— when talking about families, tell children something about your
  family – children are naturally curious about their teachers!

You may have to use one or two words of mother tongue to help children
understand, but you can then say it again, all in English.

To encourage children's **cognitive** development, you can select a range
of types of language activity.

There are seven activity types given in Activity Box A on the next page.
These

— will help develop children's thinking skills
— help the child work from the most basic use of language to
  more complex uses
— can encourage sharing and co-operation
— could form a graded sequence of speaking activities for pupils
  working in groups.

The examples in Box B show some things that small groups of children
can do in order to develop cognitive thinking and fluency in speaking –
in any language.

You can combine different types of activity. For example, you might ask
the class to compare the story endings proposed by each group.

Activity Box A
Seven activity types

1 Listing

2 Ordering and sorting

3 Matching

4 Comparing

5 Predicting and problem-solving

6 Sharing personal experiences

7 Creative work

Examples Box B
Pupils can

1 think of the names of things they can see or remember in a picture

2 classify items according to category (e.g. big animals, small animals) or put actions in a sequence

3 find pairs of similar things, or match pictures to words or numbers

4 Find what is similar and what is different in two pictures or stories

5 say what will happen in a story or decide what to do if you lose your purse or find something valuable that is not yours

6 speak about themselves and say what they like and dislike

7 do projects on chosen topics, or retell stories and make up endings.

So far in this book the activities and games have generally been of types one, two, and three. In this unit we show some slightly more challenging activities and progress to types four and six. Five and seven will come in later units.

Children as language learners

Learners need
— to hear clear pronunciation and intonation
— to feel successful when using English
— plenty of opportunities to communicate
— to enjoy their efforts at speaking in English
— to know they have achieved something worthwhile.

You as the teacher can
— speak a lot of English and repeat children's words or phrases when you are answering them
— react to the meaning of what they are trying to say
— encourage them by showing that what they are saying is more important than your correction
— wait until they finish speaking before you repeat and rephrase
— show your approval for all your pupils' speaking – however short it may be
— provide activities that are fun and that have a purpose or a goal, and that have an end-product that they can feel proud of.

Set up activities so that children can do them in pairs and groups. Then they will get opportunities to use English not just to respond to questions, but also to ask questions. They will also have the satisfaction of completing a task on their own. You can help children by
— showing them what to do first
— practising an activity first with the whole class
— arranging children into groups so that you can easily get around to listen and talk to them all.

In sections **5.2** and **5.3** we will look at activities where the teacher guides and supports the children as they speak – these are teacher-led activities. When children feel confident and happy using English, you can move to group activities so that they can speak more (see section **5.4**). As children learn to read and write they will naturally do more individual and group work – this will be covered in later units.

5 A

Talking about brothers and sisters

TEACHER: Now everyone listen to my question. Giada, have you got any brothers or sisters?

GIADA: Sister.

TEACHER: How many sisters have you got?

GIADA: Em, one.

TEACHER: One. Very good. So you've got one sister. OK, Federica, have you got any brothers or sisters?

FEDERICA: Brother ... one.

TEACHER: One brother. Good. And Francesca have you got any brothers or sisters?

FRANCESCA: Three brothers.

TEACHER: You've got three brothers! Very good.

CHILDREN: Teacher ... teacher ...

TEACHER: And, eh ... Lorenzo, have you got any brothers or sisters?

LORENZO: Three brothers.

TEACHER: Ah, you've got three brothers and have you got any sisters?

LORENZO: No.

TEACHER: No? no sisters?

OTHER CHILDREN: Yes ... yes ... yes.

TEACHER: Do you have a sister Lorenzo? How many sisters?

LORENZO: One.

TEACHER: One sister. You've got one sister. Sara. Isn't that right? Sara is your sister. OK, good Lorenzo. You've got three brothers and one sister ...

Flaviana with eight to nine year olds.

5.2   Starting to speak freely – eliciting personal talk

Children generally like to talk about themselves, and to hear their classmates doing the same. They enjoy talking about their favourite things, their hobbies, sports, families, and so on.

Listen to the teacher in **5A** asking her pupils to speak about their families. Notice that
— the children's responses are very short
— the teacher rephrases and adds to what the children say
— she praises her pupils' efforts
— the context is real and meaningful.

The context in this interaction is very clear and simple. The pupils need two types of word sets to answer:
— brother/s and sister/s
— numbers.
The context is real and the children are thinking of the meaning, not just repeating words to practise pronunciation. The communication is
— controlled because of the limitations of the language used
— more than a language exercise.

With older children you can use this teacher-led question and answer activity to do a survey of some kind, for example,
— find the average number of brothers and sisters in the class, or
— find out whether there are more boys than girls in all their families put together.
(This is more fun if you first ask them to guess whether there will be more girls than boys!) To turn this activity into a survey, draw two columns on the board, one for girls and one for boys. As children answer, write the number they say in the correct column. At the end, you can get the class to add it all up in English, and see who guessed correctly.

Extension ideas

You can follow on from this activity by asking children to
— ask questions and give short answers about each other, for example,
    How many brothers has Francesca/Federica/Giada got?
— focus on the use of *he/she*
— join the information together to prepare for more **sustained** speaking.

Personal presentation is an example of more sustained talk with older children (see **5E**).

LANGUAGE FOCUS 5.2

Initiations and follow-up moves

In **5A** Flaviana uses a typical classroom **interaction** pattern in her activity. This pattern is:
— initiation (usually a question from the teacher)
— response (an answer from the child)
— follow-up (feedback from the teacher).

a Here are two things the teacher said and a child's response, but they are mixed up. Which is an initiation, which a response, and which a follow-up? Write in I or R or F. Then say them in the correct order.
1 _____ One, very good, so you've got one sister.
2 _____ How many sisters have you got?
3 _____ One.

↻ Now read transcript **5A**. Put a <u>dotted line</u> under the teacher's initiations and a <u>solid line</u> under her follow-ups.

b In how many follow-ups does she rephrase and extend what the child has said?

🎧 Listen to the recording again, notice the intonation the teacher uses and repeat the teacher's Initiations and follow-ups.

RECORD Choose four follow-ups to record. Can you make them sound really encouraging?

TEACHING TIPS

✔ Support children's early efforts by
  — waiting for their responses (don't be afraid of silence)
  — repeating what they say in your response
  — frequently summarizing what different pupils say.

✔ Give children lots of opportunities to speak. BUT
✔ Don't put pressure on children to speak if they are not ready.
✔ Remember – silent children are still likely to be listening and learning.

TOPIC TALK
Families

↻ **1** Think of two families you know that are quite different from each other. Prepare to describe each family and compare them.

RECORD   Record what you could say about them.

2 If you were going to talk about your own family to a class of young learners around nine or ten years old, what would you tell them? What might you write or draw on the board?

3 If you were going to do the same lesson with a group of five year olds, how would you change it? Plan what you would do and say.

RECORD **4** Finally record yourself telling both classes about your family.

↻ **5** Find a story book that the children know with a story about a family. It doesn't have to be in English, but it should have pictures. Prepare questions to ask the children in English about the characters, and suggest possible answers they might make. Plan some possible follow-ups, too, e.g.
— *Who is this person? Who knows?*
— *Grandmother*
— *Yes, it's Red Riding Hood's grandmother isn't it … she's smiling and has lots of grey hair …*

RECORD   Practise these and then record three short conversations.

5.3 Speaking games

You can encourage children to use English by playing a game at the same time.

The games can be teacher-led.

Here are extracts from two classes. The children in the first class are playing 'Pass the ball' and in the second one they are playing 'Guess the mime'.

Pass the ball

To play 'Pass the ball' you need a tape recorder, a music cassette, and a ball. This is how you play it:
— Put on the music.
— The children keep passing the ball to the child next to them.
— When the music stops, the child with the ball has to answer a question or talk about a picture.
— If a child does not want to answer, he or she can say *Pass*.
— When the music starts again, the ball continues around the room.
— You can say *change* at any time and the ball will go in the opposite direction.

5 B

Pass the ball

TEACHER: Ready. Here's the music. Pass the ball.
(*Music stops.*)
TEACHER: OK, Lara tell me three things you can see in this kitchen.
LARA: A table … a chair and … a window.
TEACHER: Good, a table, a chair, and a window.
(*The music is on again and the pupils pass the ball. The music stops.*)
TEACHER: OK. Anna, can you name three things in this picture?

Lucy with eight to nine year olds.

The teacher in **5B** is showing her pupils pictures of different rooms. When the music stops the children have to name three things in the room they are looking at.

In this class the teacher is using pictures of rooms to remind the children of particular things. In this way the language is controlled by the topic. The children
— can stand in a circle or at their desks
— are listening to the music and passing the ball
— are not thinking all the time about answering in English.

Extension ideas

After playing this game you could play a memory game. The children could
— try to remember who said which things for each room
— look at the pictures again in pairs, then turn them over and name as many things as they can
— without seeing the pictures again:
  — list five things in each room
  — say what colours those things in that room were
  — say where they were.

TEACHING TIPS

✔ Use any set of words or phrases from a topic the children are familiar with.

✔ Use a story the children know well, and
— ask questions about characters
— ask what happens next.

LANGUAGE FOCUS 5.3a

Instructions for 'Pass the ball'

↻ a Read how to play 'Pass the ball'. As you read, think what you would actually say to your class when setting the game up and giving instructions for playing it. Can you continue the teacher's instructions below, using the directions above to help you?

Now, we are going to use these pictures of rooms to play a game called 'Pass the ball'. OK? So we need the ball, who can fetch the ball? OK, Kevin – wait – pass it gently, thanks. Now – we need some music …. Ah, here's a cassette. I'll just put it in. There we are. So now, everybody stand up and …

Extra phrases for ball games

b Try to think of seven verbs that are often used with the word *ball*, e.g. *roll*, *bounce*.

c Read all these phrases out loud. Which one is the least likely to be used about a ball?

Guess the mime

Miming is another activity that involves movement. It is also good fun. In Unit 2 we looked at how children can mime activities when listening. In **5C** miming is part of a speaking activity.

To play 'Guess the mime' you need some pictures of people doing different things.

Put the pictures on the board. The children can
— work in pairs
— choose any picture they like
— become the person in the picture and behave like this person
— perform the mime together.

The rest of the class watch and try to guess which activity they are miming.

They can ask the question *Are you swimming?* or just call out the names of the actions, for example, *swimming*.

5 C

Guess the mime

TEACHER: OK, now you remember what these people in the pictures are doing. OK, you're ready. Now, you two … you're going to mime. OK, everyone else – are you watching? OK, good, now off you go and guess what they're doing.
(*Two children mime together.*)

TEACHER: OK, can you guess what they're doing? Hands up anybody …

CHILDREN: Cooking …

TEACHER: Cooking. So they're cooking like this man here? Is that it? Do you want to see it again? No? Is that right?

TWO CHILDREN WHO DID THE MIME: Yes, yes cooking.

TEACHER: Yes. You're right. OK. Very good. OK, thank you very much. Next?

Brian with eight to nine year olds.

So you're holding a pan and you are stirring something… right?

TEACHING TIP

Mimes

✔ After mimes ask children to remember what different pupils were doing, e.g. *What were Kevin and David doing? Were they swimming or playing football?*

LANGUAGE FOCUS 5.3b

Asking children to guess or remember

RECORD   Practise some questions from this table, then record four.

Who can guess what	
Can you say/ask them what	they are doing?
Hands up if you can guess what	they are going to do next?
Can you remember what	Amanda and Marta were doing?

TOPIC TALK
Rooms

↻ 1 Find two or three pictures of typical rooms that your children would be familiar with, e.g. two bedrooms, two sitting rooms, or two kitchens. Look at them carefully for a minute then turn them over.

From memory describe one of them to someone else. Can she/he tell which picture you described? Afterwards, find out what made him/her sure that it was that picture.

RECORD   Without looking, talk for one minute about each picture and record your description. Play it back, looking at the picture, and check how **accurate** you were.

RECORD **2**　Record yourself describing one of the rooms. Adjust your language to suit the age and level of your learners. Make two or three deliberate errors, for example, say *there are two tables in this room and one chair instead of one table and two chairs.*

Play this recording in class and let the children look at the pictures. Ask them to spot the things that are not true. Give them time to correct what you said. This is good speaking practice.

Later your pupils could prepare a similar game to play on their own in groups of three or four. They could bring in pictures or draw them.

5.4　Children speaking in groups

The activities in sections **5.2** and **5.3** show how the teacher supports the children's speaking with lots of rephrasing and additional language.

You will find that some children
— speak more and others speak less
— are embarrassed speaking in front of the whole class
— feel more confident speaking in pairs or small groups.

When your pupils work in pairs and groups they
— get more opportunities to speak
— ask and answer questions
— learn a lot from each other
— gain confidence because they are speaking in private rather than to the whole class.

5 D

Find four differences

TEACHER: Then I want you to do pairwork. I prepared two pictures A and B. OK, so please don't show your pictures to your partner. OK? sh … sh …
(*The teacher gives out the pictures to each pair.*)
TEACHER: OK, everybody, everybody … there are four differences. There are four differences in the pictures. So please talk about the picture and find out what the four differences are. OK?
SAORI: A boy is riding a bicycle.
HIRO: No. A boy is playing soccer.
SAORI: Yes. A boy is flying a kite.
HIRO: No. A boy is playing golf.
SAORI: Pardon? Pardon?
HIRO: A boy is playing golf.
SAORI: Yes. A girl is drawing a picture.

Fumiko with ten year olds.

5 E

Personal presentation

TEACHER: OK, now start with your name and where you live.
HARUKA: My name is Haruka. I live in Ena.
TEACHER: Good. And brothers and sisters?
HARUKA: I have two brothers.
TEACHER: Good. And what do you like?
HARUKA: I like comics and cartoons.
TEACHER: OK, now tell us again. Put it all together … name, where you live, brothers, what you like, OK …
HARUKA: My name is Haruka. I live in Ena. I have two brothers.
TEACHER: And you like?
HARUKA: I like comics and cartoons.
TEACHER: Very good. Now…

Bob with eleven to twelve year olds.

🎧 Listen to the class in **5D**. The teacher has practised several 'Spot the difference' activities with her pupils in earlier lessons.
Here the children are
— working in pairs
— looking for four differences
— unable to see their partner's picture
— describing people in their own picture to see if their partner has the same
— using rising intonation as a short cut.

The intonation here is like the question *Is what I am describing the same as yours?*

This was done in a class of 22 pupils. All the pairs did the activity together. It was quite noisy – but think of the amount of practice children get when they do this.

Notice that the teacher does not interfere when the children are doing the activity.

Personal presentations

As we saw in **5A**, many teachers start by asking children about themselves: their name – where they live – their telephone number – what they like.

Pupils can extend this later to personal presentations.

🎧 Listen to this pupil in **5E** speaking about herself. Notice how the teacher helps her to build up her **presentation**.

This kind of presentation can be used in many different ways.

🎧 Listen to the pupils in **5F**. They are playing a guessing game, pretending to be a particular animal. They prepared their presentation in pairs before doing it in front of the class.

5F

Guess what animal I am

TEACHER: Now are you ready? You are going to do this all together. OK, so off you go. Who's going to start?

CHILD: Me … I am a big animal. I live out in the country. I have lots of friends. I have four feet.

TEACHER: OK.

CHILD: And I have two big ears, a small tail. I am grey. I am very big and I have a big nose. Who am I?

TEACHER: OK. Does anyone know who he is?

CHILDREN: An elephant.

Brian with eleven to twelve year olds.

In **5F** the pupils planned how to describe the animal they were going to be. This kind of self-description is like activity number 7 in Activity Box A.

To prepare for this guessing game, children could do one of these:
1 name and describe animals while looking at pictures
2 group pictures into big/small animals – wild/farm animals
3 find similarities and differences, e.g. pictures of an elephant and a mouse
4 play different guessing games. Let the children describe pictures on the walls. Ask the other groups to pick the right picture from the description
5 play **'odd one out'**
   — the children add one different category to their list
   — the others have to pick it out and say why it is the odd one out, for example, *cat, hamster, tiger, dog.*

Then the children will be familiar with phrases they can use to describe their animal for the guessing game.

Children speaking in pairs and groups

✔ Make your instructions very clear.
✔ Show the children first what you want them to do.
✔ Help them to acquire phrases to use when talking to each other

✔ Give children planning time to think of what to say.
✔ Let them rehearse if they are going to speak to all the class.

LANGUAGE FOCUS 5.4

Setting up pairs and groups

↻ **a** Read through the transcripts in this unit and take a note of all the language where instructions are given.

RECORD ↻ **b** Practise some instructions from these tables. Then record yourself giving three different sets of instructions.

Are you ready?	You're going to do this	in pairs.
OK, everyone,		in twos.
So now everybody,	You're going to work	in threes.
Quiet please!		in groups of three or four.
Listen carefully.	You will be playing this	
Here are two pictures, but don't look at them yet.	You must not show them to anyone else.	So, you two together.
Keep them face down!	Keep them like this!	You two and you three.
	You can look at them both/all together.	Go and sit with Laura please and make a pair.

Children in pairs or groups

Which of these phrases might be useful for your learners? Can you think of any more? Adapt them to suit activities your pupils could do.

Child 1	Child 2
Who wants to start?	Me!/Not me!
Whose turn is it?	Mine! Yours! Ana's!
Who's next?	Me! Ana!
You're next/I'm next!	OK.
I'll draw and you colour, OK?	Yes.
I'll ask and you answer, OK?	All right.
You first and then me, OK?	Yes!/No, you first!
Have we/you finished?	Yes!/Not yet!/Just a minute!
Can you pass me a blue pencil/a yellow crayon please?	Here you are.
Can I have the rubber/the eraser please?	Here it is!
Oh, I need the ruler/the scissors.	Here you are/Oh! wait a minute.
Who's got the red marker?	Me! Here you are/Here it is.

Pronunciation point

Connected speech. Sounds /ɒ/ and /ʌ/

1   Say these five phrases:

Have you got any (**5A**)? ... *Hands up anybody* (**5C**).
Tell us again ... Put it all ... Would you like ... (**5E**)

Do you say each word separately?
What do you notice about the sounds at the end and beginning of
the words?

2   Sort these words into two groups according to the sounds of the **stressed**
vowel:

soccer   months   comic   brother   want   mother

Further ideas

1   Prepare a guessing game. Think of two different children (a girl and
a boy) in one of your classes. Write down four or five things you could say
about each of them (their families, what they like, etc.).

RECORD   Record yourself talking about them. Take your recordings into class and
play them to all the children. Can anyone guess which of them you are
talking about? Do not give them the answers straight away. You might
need to play the recording two or three times. If they say a name, ask
them why they think it is that child.

2   Write down what you have learnt from doing this unit. What do you feel
you want more help with?

3   Read the Introduction and Chapter 6, 'Role plays and improvisation', in
Philips, Sarah. 1999. *Drama with Children.* Oxford: Oxford University
Press, OR
Chapter 6 in **Moon, Jayne. 2000.** *Children Learning English.* Oxford:
Macmillan Heinemann.

6

Reading in English

Introduction

In previous units we have focused on
— listening as the main source of language
— how speaking activities can be started and developed.
All the activities we have looked at in these chapters could be extended to include reading practice.

> **Think about**
> how ...
> — all children listen from birth and naturally **acquire** speech.
> — all children have to learn how to read and write.
> — if children's mother tongue is written in roman script, you can use a teaching method that focuses on meaning from the beginning.
> — if children have a mother tongue that is not based on roman script, then you will have to spend some time on sounds, letter shape, and word recognition.
> — meaning is the most important element in reading just as it is in listening.
> — just as listening came before speaking, so reading comes before writing.

> **Think about**
> your own teaching situation.
> — How old are the children in your class?
> — Can they read and write in their mother tongue?
> — Do they know the roman script?
> — Do they know there are different spellings for similar sounds in English, e.g. *show, sugar* – /ʃ/?
> — What words might beginners recognize already?

↻ Look at the list in the box below. What are your three main priorities when teaching your pupils to read in English?

> **Priorities when teaching reading and writing**
> — focus on meaning
> — word recognition
> — making the connection between familiar sounds and written words or phrases
> — naming the letters of the alphabet
> — predicting the pronunciation of a written word

Look back at the aims for 'listening and doing' activities at the beginning of Unit 2. In the same way as you help children develop listening strategies through suitable activities, you can help them develop reading strategies.

For example, children
— can 'read and do', so give them short written instructions on cards
to follow, for example, *Point to the window*…
— can use other clues to understand the written word, such as pictures
and sounds
— do not need to understand everything fully, they just need to
understand the key words and general meaning.

6.1 Beginning reading

You know best about your teaching situation. Do your pupils know how
to read in their own language? This is a big step because children have to
understand the association between what they hear and what they read.

Do you teach reading in English in the same way as you teach reading
in your mother tongue? Learning to read in English is not as difficult if
children can read in their own language, even if it is written in a
different script. Your teaching situation is the most important factor
when deciding how you should teach reading.

There are two main approaches to teaching reading in English.

Look and say

Teachers often use 'look and say' as part of vocabulary teaching. So when
children learn to say a new word they learn to read it. You can help
children with whole word recognition by using printed material as much
as you can in your classroom, e.g. word cards used for labelling and
directions. Of course, the new words are learnt in **context**.

This can also be done with phrases. Children use the same recognition
skills when they are remembering a word or a short phrase.

In 6.2 we will listen to a teacher using 'look and say' techniques to
teach some new words.

Phonics (letters used to make sounds)

English spelling is difficult. Children need to learn how to recognize sounds and letters. It is better not to teach the names of letters when starting to teach reading, as of course some of the letters of the English alphabet no longer match the actual sounds of the language. When you use phonics, you are teaching children the way the letter sounds, not the name of the letter.

Young learners

— can learn obvious letter patterns that help with sound recognition and help them predict words, for example, *shop, jam,* etc.
   Visual clues make words and phrases easier to remember.
— will not need to know the formal names of the letters until they start to write and spell.

Another way to help children with sounds is to let them play with the sounds as they repeat a word they are reading on a card or in their book, e.g. singing it or saying it loudly or quickly or slowly, or whispering.

This playing with words obviously helps pronunciation but it also helps children remember the word.

Many teachers use both 'look and say' and **phonics**. And you can use both of these with more meaningful material such as story books. (We will look at stories in Units 8 and 9.)

Activities to help children connect sounds with letters

Children whose first language is written in roman script can learn the first letter of their own name and look for their 'special words':

Ana – apple, art.

Let children with non-roman script names pick their favourite thing/colour/animal and use the first letter as their special letter:

panda – pocket – picture.

Play alphabet games:
— memory games – using letter cards

— initial letter games – children recognize and collect the first letters of different words:

What letter does mango *begin with?*
— feel the letter – children close their eyes and touch cut-out sandpaper letters on a card. *Find the 't' for tiger.*

— Make an alphabet **frieze** with card spaces underneath for lots of extra words that children can recognize and read.

Activities to help children connect sound recognition with clusters of written letters

— Make children **aware** of the patterns in
   — final word endings that rhyme in songs and chants
   — games and songs with a focus on beginning sounds
   — displays or games that emphasize a particular sound.
— Help them focus on visual sound patterns, for example, *pl* cluster in *plant – planet – plane*, and the *st* cluster in *star – stamp – story*.
— Talk about these patterns with the children – help them to see how they can use this awareness to guess words.
— Let children point to these patterns/words when you are all reading something together.
— Colour or highlight these patterns on word cards.

You can connect many of these activities with writing and with the activities we are going to look at in Units 8–9 on stories.

LANGUAGE FOCUS 6.1

Letter and word recognition

a **'Look and say' approach**

↻ To do this exercise, have two or three sets of flashcards with words on them, for example, *animal words, colour words, sports words*.

Look at the table on the next page. It has some instructions you can use with a 'look and say' approach to reading, for example, *Who can find their favourite food or drink? Pick it up and show us.*

Use the table to make six different instruction patterns. You can adapt them and add to them. Now practise them with someone else.

RECORD   Then record them.

Can you find your	name card on the table?	Pick it up and show us …
		Can you put it on your desk?
Who can find their	favourite colour among these words?	Can you read it out to us?
		Good – can you tell us what it says?
	favourite food or drink?	How many other colour words can you read?
Who can find	a word for a colour?	What other animal words can you read?
	the word for 'blue'?	What does this one say?
	the card which says 'blue'?	
	a card with an animal name on?	

b Phonic approach

↻ Do the same with these tables. Add to them, too.

OK – let's see how many letters you can remember. Who can find a letter which says 'h'? Yes – 'h' like for your name, Hiro … or 'h' for happy or hungry. Who is hungry? Anyone? OK, so who can point to the letter for 'h'?

Who can	find	a letter which says *ssss*	like a *ssssnake* like in your name, Sam?
Can you	point to	a word beginning with a *w* sound	as in *wolf*?
Can anyone	see	a word that starts with a *b*	like b for *banana*?
		the letters for a *th* sound	like you get in *three*?
		a word that ends with a *n* sound	like *green, man*?
		a word that rhymes with *cat*	like *hat, sat*?

c Words children already know or half-know from their mother tongue

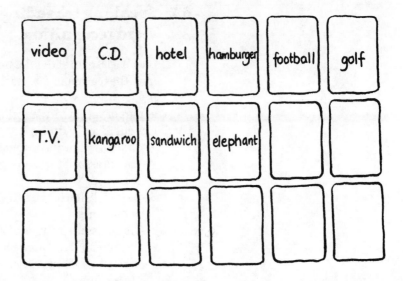

↻   Write on the blank cards other words your pupils may be familiar with, and
    will not have too much trouble reading.
       Then use these instructions to plan four different things to ask children
    to do with these cards.

RECORD   Practise and record them, giving an example each time.

Choose	any words for food.	Put all the food words together in a circle/list.
	any words for drink.	
Find	three words for sports.	Draw a picture for three of them.
Read out loud	four words from the song we've just sung.	Match each word to a picture.
Come out and take down	any words from the rhyme we've just said.	Find a picture to go with each word.
Team A come and find		Where are you going to put this word? Beside the …?
Team B come and take	three words you like best.	Where does this word go?
		How many are there left?

d   What does it say?

In English, when talking about what is written down, we nearly always use
the word *say*. In the examples below, decide which word is likely to be
stressed, then practise saying these questions out loud. Choose five to
record, and give a sample answer.

— *What does it say on this card/label?*
— *What does this sign say? IN or OUT?*
— *What does this word say? What's this one?*
— *What does this letter say? What sound does it make?*
— *What do these letters say when they are together?*
— *What sound do these letters make together?*
— *What sound does this word start with (end with)?*
— *What other words start with (end with) that sound?*
— *Look, there's an e on the end, so does it say* bite *or* bit*?*

6.2   Speaking to reading – helping sound and word recognition

Look back again at the classroom extracts **4E** (page 49) and **4G** (page 52).
Jane, the teacher in that class, was helping her pupils remember and
pronounce new vocabulary. In **6A** we hear Jane using 'word reading'
as part of vocabulary learning.
Her pupils are learning
— about rhythm and **intonation** as they learn new words
— how to associate meaning and sound with the written word when
   they read.
Before you listen to the extract, read this summary of the class
activities. Jane
— first sticks up pictures of the six words on the board
— then uses a tambourine to beat out the rhythm of the new words
— then says a chant with the children using the new words they
   are learning.

6 A

Using a tambourine for rhythm and syllable work

TEACHER: Good. Now, thank you. OK, one more thing … Let's see who can tell me … Who can tell me this one? Listen.
(*The teacher beats twice on the tambourine.*)

TEACHER: OK, hands up. Listen. Now listen.
(*The teacher beats twice on the tambourine again.*)

CHILDREN: Planet …

TEACHER: Yeah yeah … plan … et. Could be planet, couldn't it? Anything else? … star?

CHILDREN: No.

TEACHER: Rainbow? Yes?

CHILDREN: Yes.

TEACHER: Yes look … plan … et … rain … bow …
(*The teacher beats twice on the tambourine.*)

TEACHER: Or how about this one then?
(*The teacher beats once on the tambourine.*)

TEACHER: Moon?

CHILDREN: Yes … yes.

TEACHER: Star …

CHILDREN: Yes … yes.

TEACHER: Yes and it could be sun and it could be cloud. Now I'm going to choose one and you have to guess which word this is …
(*The teacher beats once on the tambourine.*)

CHILDREN: Star.

TEACHER: Could be … What else?

CHILDREN: Moon.

TEACHER: Yes. Now, Laura you come out and choose one. OK.
(*Different children take turns to choose a word and give the correct number of beats on the tambourine.*)

Jane with seven to eight year olds.

🎧 Now listen to **6A**. Jane
— focuses the children's attention on the syllabic beat of the words
— **elicits** the number of **syllables** in the words they are learning
— lets individual children beat out the syllables of the remaining words
— asks other children to guess the word.

LANGUAGE FOCUS 6.2

Encouraging learner participation

a Read transcript **6A**. Find six different phrases that Jane uses to get the children to do this particular activity. (Note: only the ones that are just for this activity so NOT phrases like *Hands up*. You use that phrase with lots of activities.) Try saying these phrases with a suitable intonation. Mark the words in each phrase that you think carry the main **stress**.

🎧 Listen to **6A** on the CD again and repeat these phrases as they are said.

RECORD Finally, record them on to your cassette.

Asking children to guess the word

b Read these ten phrases out loud. Which one is probably not about guessing or predicting?
— You have to guess which word this is.
— What do you think this could be?
— Now what about this one?
— It starts with *r* so it might be …
— It's something that's in her basket, so what might this be?
— It could be a …
— Let's put everything away.
— Think of the story – so what could this be about?
— What else could it be?
— What do you think?

6 B

Matching words to pictures

TEACHER: Now put everything away.
We're going to do something else.
We're going to do something else.
OK … sh … sh …

TEACHER: Now what do you think this
is? Mm … hm …

CHILD: Planet … planet.

TEACHER: OK, then, Irene, come and get
it. Let's see where it's going to go. OK,
where are you going to put it?
(*The pupil puts the word beside the
matching picture.*)

TEACHER: OK. Beside the picture of the
planet. Very good. Now what about
this one?
(*They go through all the words
and each word is put beside the
matching picture.*)

Jane with seven to eight year olds.

6 C

Recognizing the correct word

TEACHER: Now do you want to help me?
Em … this is rainbow?

CHILDREN: No.

TEACHER: Erm … Moon?

CHILDREN: No.

TEACHER: Erm … Cloud?

CHILDREN: Yes.

Jane with seven to eight year olds.

6 D

Reading words

TEACHER: Now let's see if we can do …
Do you remember the game 'clever
parrot'? If it's the same, what
should you do?

CHILDREN: Say it.

TEACHER: Say it.
(*Some children comment in their
mother tongue also.*)

TEACHER: OK, now look at the card …
OK? Rainbow, moon, sun, star …

ALL THE CHILDREN: Star!

Jane with seven to eight year olds.

🎧 Listen to **6B**. The children are now matching the written word to the
picture on the board. Jane asks the children
— to look at the words on cards
— to put them beside the matching picture on the blackboard.

🎧 Now listen to **6C**. Jane
— holds the cards in front of her so that the children can see them
— doesn't look at the cards
— says one of the words.
The children have to say if she is right or wrong. Listen to them
doing this.

🎧 In **6D** the pupils are playing a game. The game is called 'clever parrot'.
The children have to repeat like a parrot. But they must be clever parrots
and only repeat the word on the card. The teacher
— shows a card to the pupils
— doesn't look at the card
— repeats all the words.

The children have to
— look and listen carefully
— repeat the word that is on the card when they hear it.

To finish this lesson Jane plays a fast word-reading game.
— She uses the word cards again.
— She turns over a word card very quickly.
— The children only see it for a second.
— They call out the word they read.

You could use some of these activities
— when teaching new vocabulary
— when you want to **revise** or go over vocabulary the children
  learnt before
— before children read a story or say a rhyme which includes
  these words.

Summary of the pre-reading activities

The activities we have listened to here show how you can
— focus on new words in context
— teach sound and letter/word recognition at the same time
— get children to match sound and written forms
— repeat constantly to teach pronunciation
— let children have fun while learning to read.

Extension ideas

— Play label games with groups or whole class, e.g. remove all the labels
  you use in class and get the children to stick them all back on again.
— Play word games
    — use sets of words the children are already familiar with, e.g. fruit,
      animals, or characters from stories
    — guess what's missing/odd one out/dominoes/snap/bingo.
— Get children to think about and remember words by using a password
  for the class. Every day someone can choose a new password. During
  the day you can remind everyone of this word and then make it the
  password for the next morning.

Word recognition

- ✔ **Label** things in the classroom, even pictures/photos that you use.
- ✔ Keep sets of pictures and new words and phrases children have learnt recently in a special **display** area.
- ✔ Let the children play at being teacher to revise these words and phrases.

- ✔ Hand out wishes cards and praise cards with short phrases that children can bring home and read to their parents, e.g.
  Wishes cards *Have a nice weekend … See you Monday.*
  Praise cards *Well done … Fantastic … Thank you for a nice meal …*

TOPIC TALK
Holidays/vacations

1 With a colleague, complete the following **mind map**.
There are five connected bubbles. You might like to add others.
The questions you need to ask have been left out.

What five questions would you ask?
For other mind-map ideas see the Website references on page 142.

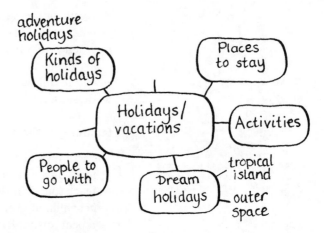

2 Think about the best holiday/worst vacation you have ever had. Why was it so good/bad? Prepare to tell someone else about it.

RECORD Record yourself talking about this.

6.3 Helping children recognize phrases

Children **acquire** words and phrases when they listen. As they become familiar with phrases in English they are unconsciously learning about word order. When they start to read and later to write, you can do activities
— that consolidate what they have heard and show them the same patterns, written down
— that allow children to slowly become **aware** of word order.

Listen to the teacher in **6E** helping his class with phrase reading from the story *Little Red Riding Hood*. He is using word cards for the things in Red Riding Hood's basket. The children already know the story and have heard the phrases before.

This lesson is based on a story, but you can use reading material from many sources. One of the best sources of early reading material is what the children make up themselves.

Let children make reading cards. They can colour and illustrate them. You can
— write down what the children say
— let the children make the cards slowly
— let everyone in the class make a card
— keep the cards in pockets with the children's names on the outside
— use what the children have written for word/phrase recognition activities.

6 E

Building a phrase

TEACHER: OK, everybody, look carefully. Here are all the things in Red Riding Hood's basket. But the words are all mixed up. So we're going to sort them out. OK, right, right who can remember what she had?

CHILDREN: Strawberries.

TEACHER: Strawberries, yes. Strawberries … good. Who can come out and find the word for strawberries?

CHILDREN: Me, me …

TEACHER: OK, Leah. OK. Yes, good. And what were the strawberries like? They were lovely …

CHILDREN: Sweet … sweet …

TEACHER: Yes. They were lovely sweet strawberries. So who can find these words?

CHILD: Me.

TEACHER: OK, Ali. And where do they go? Put them next to the strawberries. Which one goes first? That's right? That's right. Good, let's read that phrase together …

CHILDREN AND TEACHER: Lovely … sweet … strawberries.

TEACHER: lovely sweet strawberries. Mm. Yes.

Brian with eight to nine year olds.

TEACHING TIPS

✔ Make up group chants based on what the children already know and using the phrases the children can read out:

What's in the basket?	Lovely sweet strawberries
What's in the wood?	Small blue flowers
What's in the bed?	The big bad wolf
What's in his mouth?	His big sharp teeth
What's in his tummy?	Not me, not me!!

✔ Pick out phrases that you can use for matching games from reading material
✔ Use picture cards and cards with labels or short phrases or descriptions. Ask the children to find the picture to match the writing.

Which monster is this? My monster has two heads, four feet, two hands, 6 fingers, and big smiles.

Extension ideas

— Put phrases based on topics/stories that the children know on reading cards. Let them put the cards together in various combinations to make sentences.

He's   This is   in my house   sometimes   a lot   running

Charlie   my dog   He lives   He barks   I like him   He loves

— Take suitable phrases out of stories to make substitution games and sequencing games, like this one for Cinderella.

the frog the pumpkin the mice	changed into	a coach horses a coachman

First group	Second group	Last group of cards
The snake	are buying	a bicycle
The kangaroo	is riding	an aeroplane
		a hamburger

LANGUAGE FOCUS 6.3

Making phrases or sentences

After talking about pictures or reading a story, you can write words or sentence halves on separate cards, like the ones above, and ask children to do one of these activities.

Use your own flashcards and practise two or three sets of instructions for these.

Make phrases using the words on these cards — *lovely red strawberries* OR *lovely sweet apples*.	They should be true ones.	And then read them to your partner.
	They can be true or false.	He/she can say if they are true or not true.
Make sentences using the phrases on your cards — *The mice changed into horses.*	They can be silly ones.	Ask him/her if it was quite silly or very silly.

⌕ Pronunciation point

Sounds /ɔː/ and /ɜː/

⚬ Do you remember how these words were pronounced in class extracts in this unit and in earlier units?

1 *walk, work, shirt, talk, words*. Put them in two groups according to the vowel sound.

2 And what group does the word *sort* go in?

RECORD Either record yourself or work with a partner and say these pairs of words and some more pairs:

walk work … work work … work walk … walk walk …

Play back your recording or get someone to listen to you and decide if the pairs you have said are the same or different.

6.4 Reading independently – finding information

— When children can read they can use the printed word as an alternative source of English.

— When children can read silently on their own they are developing confidence and independence.

— To check their pronunciation, ask individual pupils to read a little bit out loud for you.

— Children should always have time to look at a written text before reading it aloud.

> REMEMBER
> — **Prediction** is an important part of our thinking process. Children need to practise thinking about and guessing what comes next.
> — Children can learn to predict what a word means from
>   — **context**,
>   e.g. *initial sound combined with general meaning*
>   — pictures,
>   e.g. *illustrations in books*
>   — what they know about a topic
>   — what follows words such as *but, so, because*
>   — what they have noticed before.
> — When you encourage children to talk about what they have read you show them that their reading is important.

Helping children to be independent readers is also very practical; for example, they can tell other children what they have read.

🎧 Listen to the teacher in **6F**, Emi, getting a pupil to explain what she has read to her classmates.

6 F

Reading and transferring information

TEACHER: OK, now em … page …
OK please open your workbook …
page twenty-two.
    Now, can you read it on your own and tell me what you have to do?
(*Children reading on their own*)

TEACHER: OK, Ana can you explain what you have to do in this activity?
(*Ana explains in her mother tongue.*)

TEACHER: Do you all understand?

CHILDREN: Yes.

TEACHER: OK, do it on your own and when you've finished compare your work with your partner's. When you've finished, but not before. OK … em … perhaps five minutes, that's all.

Emi with eleven to twelve year olds.

┌───

LANGUAGE FOCUS 6.4

Chunking

Chunking means recognizing what words in a text belong together. This helps children read in meaningful phrases, not word by word.

↻ Read the Teacher's part of **6F** out loud, dividing it into short **chunks**.

🎧 Listen to it again on the CD and repeat the teacher's part.

Finding the place

Add to or adapt the table below.

RECORD Record yourself giving four sets of instructions from it.

You need your	coursebook	page 13	Read what it says …
Please open your	activity book	page 22	Can you read it on your own?
Find where we got to last time – in your	workbook	page 30	
	reader	middle of page 14	Can you do what it says?
Find your place in your			

└───

Extension ideas

Set tasks for children so that they have to read to complete them, e.g. *Read two reading cards and tell everyone what they were about. Read a set of instructions and make something, such as a Lego house.* Encourage children to read something to their parents.

> **TEACHING TIPS**
>
> **Encouraging children to develop as readers**
>
> ✔ Have a reading area in the classroom with good picture books and reading cards with pictures (see Units 8 and 9 on stories).
> ✔ Have reading material written by you and the children.
> ✔ Have simple information cards or books about other countries.
> ✔ If you have audio books (cassettes of stories) in your school, let the children read and listen at the same time.
> ✔ Play games where reading is needed to find out information, such as treasure hunt clues.

Further ideas

RECORD **1** Choose two short texts from your coursebooks suitable for your pupils and record yourself reading them out loud as you would read them to your pupils. Play them back and listen to see how expressive you are when reading.

⟳ **2** Look in your coursebooks for reading activities you can try in class. Also check the Teacher's Book to see what it says about these activities. Now plan what you would say in English to set them up in your class. Use some of the extension ideas to teaching tips in this unit.

RECORD Then record yourself in class teaching these activities.

3 Read Chapter 7 from **Brewster, Jean, Gail Ellis, and Denis Girard. 1992.** *The Primary English Teacher's Guide*. London: Penguin AND/OR Chapter 7 from **Moon, Jayne. 2000.** *Children Learning English*. Oxford: Macmillan Heinemann.

7

Writing in English

This unit looks at

activities that
- help children to learn and practise handwriting
- link writing with reading, listening, and speaking
- help children to write more freely.

Introduction

All the activities we looked at in the last unit can lead into writing activities. Here are some examples:

Reading activities using reading cards	Writing activities
1 matching words/phrases with pictures	1 copy/write from memory the word/phrase that matches the picture
2 labelling pictures or objects	2 write a label
3 predicting from initial sounds	3 finish the word st__
4 re-arranging jumbled letters to make a word	4 write the whole word
5 classifying words into sets	5 copy/write the names of all the people in the story
6 ordering sentences in the correct sequence	6 copy/write out the story in the right order
7 guessing the missing word	7 copy the phrase/sentence putting in the missing word
8 games that involve recognizing words and meaning	8 bingo, writing races

Activities like this can prepare children for more creative writing.

Handwriting

We have to remember two things that make a great difference when children are learning to write in English:
— their age
— their degree of familiarity with roman script.
When children write, they have to pay attention to several things at the same time:
— develop finger control and be tidy
— form letters
— become familiar with the relationship between sound and spelling in English
— keep the picture of the letters in their minds
— learn when to use capital letters and how to punctuate.

7A

Singing the alphabet song and writing the alphabet

TEACHER: OK, now let's sit down at the table and you need to get your pencils. Put your bags on the floor. Good, that's it. Put your bag on the floor. And now …

CHILDREN: (*singing alphabet song*) *a b c d e f g h i j k l m n o p q r s t u v w x y* and *z* …

Happy, happy, I am happy, I can do my *a b c*.

TEACHER: That's right. Now you need to write. OK. Yes, sit down at the table erm … Has anyone got a pencil? Good, good and you need …

TEACHER: There's a pencil. There you are. (*Teacher hands pencil to a child and child thanks teacher.*)

TEACHER: You're welcome. (*There is lots of mother tongue talk in this class. The teacher explains quickly and the children talk. They are about to start an alphabet writing session and the teacher is going around looking at what each child is writing.*)

TEACHER: Good. Oh good. That's a good *c*!

CHILD: Thank you.

TEACHER: Oh, how about purple?

CHILD: Teacher …

TEACHER: Uh huh. Here's little purple. There you are.

Oh good *a* Midori! How are you?

MIDORI: I'm fine.

TEACHER: Good. Who knows *d*? Oh good *d* Miroshi! Yes. Good.

Erin with four to five year olds.

Using computers

Since many children are now using electronic aids/computers, they need to
— learn the keyboard layout
— learn how to type, ideally using all their fingers and sitting properly
— learn some English expressions for using a computer/email.

Writing

Like the other three language skills, writing is about meaning.

Early writing activities such as copying, tracing, and making letter shapes are handwriting practice.

Finding the letters for computer work is a matter of recognition and developing keyboard skills.

But children always have to think about the meaning of what they are writing.

And whatever the lesson focus is – handwriting practice or keyboard skills or expressing meaning, or a combination – children should enjoy the activity and feel successful.

7.1 Practising the alphabet

In Unit 6 on reading, we looked at the letters from the point of view of the sounds they can make. For writing and learning how to spell, children may need to know the formal names of the letters and the order of the alphabet. This also helps them look up words in a dictionary.

Listen to the very young learners in **7A** (you heard them before in **2A**). Their teacher uses a lot of singing in class and the children are singing as they do their *a b c*.

These very young learners enjoy
— singing the alphabet song
— making the letters
— writing in different colours
— chatting in their mother tongue while doing their writing.

Notice how the teacher praises and comments on the children's writing.

LANGUAGE FOCUS 7.1a

Politeness phrases

This teacher is very aware of the need to be polite both inside and outside the classroom. She uses *please* and *thank you* a lot, as well as language that is typical of conversations outside the classroom.

Can you also find:

a an example of a child responding socially to a compliment (praise)

b one exchange where a child responds using a polite social phrase. (*Clue*: It is a three-part exchange, i.e. where the teacher initiates, a child responds, and the teacher follows up.)

7B

An alphabet writing race

TEACHER: OK, put your bag under your
  chair. Now two teams over here.
  One team this way. Good. One, two,
  three, OK. Eh, Keiko, what's your
  team's name?

KEIKO: Pink.

TEACHER: OK, the pink team. And Maya
  what's your team's name?

MAYA: Orange.

TEACHER: OK, the orange team. Now
  do you know what we are going to
  do? You're going to write the *a b c*.
  Now one person at a time. *a* first and
  then back to the end of the line and
  the next one writes *b* and back to the
  end of the line and you have to do the
  whole thing until you're finished.
  The whole … *a b c d e f g h* … all the
  way to *z*. So, er, here's a marker. Oh no,
  they're bad. Oh, let's use crayons.
  Ah, now pink and orange. OK, ready …
  Good, up behind the line. Come on.
  Good. One, two, three go. Now *a*
  first …

Erin with four to five year olds.

A writing race

🎧 Listen to Erin's class in **7B**.

Later in the same class the teacher has a writing race. In this way she
— continues the focus on writing practice
— varies the activity
— allows the children to be physically active.

LANGUAGE FOCUS 7.1b

Intonation and stress for meaning

1 The instruction *put your bag under your chair* in **7B** can have at least four
  different meanings according to which word you put the **stress** on.
  For example, if you mean *not under **someone else's** chair* you would say
  *Put your bag under **your** chair*.

↻ Say it three more times so that it has each of these meanings:
  a not *on* your chair
  b not under your *table*
  c don't just leave it *beside your chair*, where someone might fall over it.

⚲ Which one do you think the teacher meant in this classroom?
  Work with a colleague and choose different ways of saying this
  instruction. Can your colleague tell which meaning you gave it?

RECORD Record yourself saying it four different ways and adding on a second phrase
  to support your children, for example, *Put your bag under **your** chair, **not
  under someone else's/Taro's***.
  This kind of stress is called 'contrastive stress'.

⚲ **2** Now find these phrases in **7B**. Underline the words where you think the
  teacher put the main stress, and say why, e.g. *the **pink** team* (not another
  colour, or orange)

  — the orange team   — you have to do the whole thing
  — now, one person at a time   — all the way to *z*
  — the next one writes *b*   — let's use crayons.
    (maybe two stresses here)

In some classes you might go on to explain in words what you mean, by rephrasing the instruction and adding *not* ....

Practise doing this by finding a phrase that goes with one of the instructions above, and saying them both, one after the other, e.g. *You have to do the whole thing – not just up to 'p'.*

— not just the first half of the alphabet
— not markers – they've dried up
— not all of you together
— not just up to *p*
— not the pink team
— because *b* comes after *a*

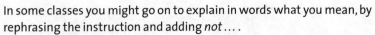 ## Pronunciation point

1 What sound?

Say the following words. What sound do the syllables in *italics* have in common?

ta*ble*, wel*come*, *about*, pur*ple*, un*der*, mar*ker*, cray*on*, al*pha*bet, remem*ber*, col*oured*, ex*er*cise, to*gether*, hap*pens*

These words are in the different extracts in this unit. This is a very common sound in English and is spelt in many different ways.

2 Sounds /iː/ and /ɪ/

Say the following words. What vowel sound is the odd one out?

team   need   sit   piece   see   eat

RECORD Record yourself or work with a partner and say these pairs of words:
it, eat ...   eat, eat ...   it, it ...   eat, it ...

TEACHING TIPS

Writing the alphabet

✔ Practise letter shapes by
  — tracing over dot letters
  — using letters cut out of rough paper and stuck on cards
— tracing the shape in the air – air writing
— asking children to put their names or initials on their drawings and other artwork.

Extension ideas

Palm-writing: feel the shape and say the letter.
— Let children work in pairs.
— The first child has the letter.
— The second child closes his/her eyes.
— The first child draws the letter outline on the palm of the second child's hand.
— The second child says the letter.

Back writing – feel the shape and write the letter
— Let children work in pairs.
— The first child has the letter/short word.
— He/She draws the outline on the second child's back.
— The second child writes down the letter or short word.
— They check together.

Keyboard preparation – finding letters and putting them in order
— Let the children work in pairs.
— Give each pair a set of alphabet cards with capital letters (you could prepare these on the computer).
— Call out the letters in the sequence they appear on the keyboard your children will be using. The children have to put them in order – but not all at once!
— Start with four letters from the centre row.
— Continue with the rest of the letters from this row.
— Then move to the top row and then to the bottom row.
— Let the children play with the letters, for example, mix up four letters first, then mix up one row at a time, and put them in sequence again.

7.2 From speaking to writing and from reading to writing

From speaking to writing: making memory games and quizzes

When children can physically make the letters of the alphabet or use a keyboard, they can do activities to practise their writing, e.g. tracing by hand, finishing words, or copying by hand or on the computer.

But as meaning is the most important aim of writing, it is always important to link these activities with what children already know and what they are learning.

> **REMEMBER**
> Children should write about what they have talked about or read about.
> You can use listening, speaking, and reading activities to prepare for their written work.

Writing for someone else, not just the teacher, is important. For example, children can write puzzles or quizzes for another pair or team to do. And with computers they can send these to other groups in their school and in other schools. This gives a purpose to writing.

Look again at classroom extract **5E** (page 62).
— The children were talking about themselves – where they live – what they like.
— When pupils finish this kind of activity you can ask them in pairs to write down two descriptions they remember.
— They don't write the name, just the description, for example, *She has two brothers and no sisters and she likes comics and cartoons. Who is she?*
— They can then read it out (or give it to another group to read) and let the others guess who it is.

Extension ideas

Memory game

Children in pairs can write, on a piece of paper, the same descriptions but leave one or two gaps, instead of writing the words. They pass it to another pair to read and fill in.

Question and answer

Children in pairs write, on a piece of paper, two or three questions about a picture they can all see. The teacher then takes the picture down, and they give their questions to another pair to answer from memory, in writing.

From reading to writing: making lists

Read the poem 'A party at Croco Bay'.

....

A PARTY AT CROCO BAY

Come to Croc's party at Croco Bay
Wonderful things are on today
There are lollipops, toffees, peppermint
      canes
Things to drink and lots of games
We'll play bingo, football, hide and seek
And we'll have fun for a whole week
The bat, the monkey and the hedgehog
The snake, the kangaroo and the frog

Are all coming to the feast
To the great party of the beasts
On the merry-go-round and on
      the swing
All the animals in a ring
They hop, they run, they jump around
They play on trees and on the ground
Croc is happy and Al is fine
See, they're all good friends of mine.

....

Listen to Flaviana and her pupils in **7C**. You have already listened to them in other units. In this class, the children

— have been reading this rhyme about Croc's party in their coursebook
— understand the 'party' vocabulary because they know the story
— are looking for words about food
— are going to underline other sets of words, for example, *animals, games* so they can write them out later.

7C

Finding words and making lists

TEACHER: OK. What is the rhyme about? It's about Croc's party. Now, look again at the rhyme and underline. What is underline?

CHILD: Under.

TEACHER: Uh uh …

CHILD: The word … here …

TEACHER: Uh uh …
   (*Lots of children say what they think.*)

TEACHER: Yes draw a line under the word … like this. So now underline all the words that have to do with food. OK. So, on your own in the rhyme you underline all the words that have to do with food. OK?

CHILDREN: Yes … yeah.
   (*Later*)

TEACHER: OK, did you find all the food? … all the food in the rhyme? OK let's write it. Erm … What did you find Giulia?

GIULIA: Lollipops.

TEACHER: Lollipops. Very good. I'll write lollipops on the board. And Federica, what did you find?

Flaviana with nine to ten year olds.

LANGUAGE FOCUS 7.2a

Reading and talking with expression

1 Listen to **7C** again, and this time, talk along WITH the teacher, trying to mirror her **stress** and **intonation**. Try this two or three times.

2 Practise reading the rhyme out loud, making it sound as dramatic and exciting as you can.

RECORD   Record yourself doing this, and play it back.
   How does it sound?

Extension ideas

After this kind of activity, the teacher could play a memory challenge game.
— Write the words on the board in separate lists, for example, *food, things they can do at the party*, etc.
— Ask the children to look carefully at the lists and try to remember them.
— Rub out the lists (or just some of the words from each list).
— Ask the children to work in groups of three or four and write out as many words as they can remember from a particular list.

This is exactly what Cristina does in her class. Listen to **7D**.

7 D

Remembering vocabulary sets and spelling

TEACHER: OK, sh ... sh ... sh ... listen please. Stay in your teams and sit down together at your tables. What you are going to do now is ... now listen ... very very carefully. I'm going to give you a piece of paper and put your group name on the top. OK.

Now, you are going to work together to try and remember these words. I'm going to write some of the words we read today on the blackboard and you have to look very carefully at the words because this is a writing competition.

Let's see if your team can remember all the words. When I write up the words look at them and remember. Now when I rub them off try to write as many words as you can. But not the same as the rest of the team. Work together in your team. (*There is lots of mother tongue talk as children explain to one another.*)

TEACHER: Very good. Now you all understand what you have to do? OK, don't write yet. Can you see the board?

Cristina with nine to ten year olds.

LANGUAGE FOCUS 7.2b

Useful phrases for group writing

Read transcript **7D**. Find the following and practise saying them fast:
— four sentences with *going to* in the first half of the extract
— six expressions that have to do with working as a group (look for phrases with the words *team, group, together*)
— two sentences with *what* clauses (one near the start and one near the end).

1 Look at the list of phrases below. Find two pairs that are opposite in meaning and one odd one out.

a So, on your own.	d Look at them and remember.
b I'll rub them off.	e Let's write up the words.
c Work together in your team.	

Spelling

Spelling is a link between reading and writing.

Today, with more telephone communication, people often have to spell names and addresses out loud.

LANGUAGE FOCUS 7.2c

Phrases with *spell*

2 Practise the phrases below.
Mark the phrases
— that might be useful for children to learn to say when in pairs or groups with a **C**
— that are useful for a teacher with a **T**. (Some might be useful for both.)

a Who knows how to spell *flowers*?	d Can you help me with my spelling?
b Who can spell out this word?	e Can you just check that spelling?
c How do you spell *enough*?	f Can you spell that for me, please?
	g I don't know how to spell *strawberries*.

RECORD Practise four teacher phrases and four learner phrases and record them on your cassette.

Extension ideas

A questioning game

— Get each child to write down (in secret) a word they can see in the classroom. (If they label things in the classroom you will have a lot of words on the walls.)
— The whole class can then play a question game (spoken or written) to guess the word. They can either say the questions, or write them and give them to the teacher or another child to read out loud.

Linking with other skills

✔ Use a new password each day in class. Ask children to write it the day before so they learn it and can say how it is spelt in their next class.

TOPIC TALK
Parties

With a colleague, plan a class party. Work out how the children can help you plan a party as a class project. Think of things you could talk about in English, read about, and write about in class. What food and games would you have? Would you invite a visitor/s? Who? Why?

7.3 Writing with other children

So far in this unit, we have focused on writing individual words, phrases, and single sentences. But children also need help in writing longer, continuous pieces of writing, such as recipes or short stories. You can use a familiar story as a basis for a class writing activity.

When children work together as a class, they can learn to help one another and co-operate.

In this section the children are writing about a story they know. They are not just going over language – they are also learning how to write a story.

Children know a lot about stories. They understand the structure, that stories have a beginning and a middle where you tell what happens, and that there are different ways to end. Children can be quite sophisticated in the way they tell stories. This is part of the knowledge they bring to class.

See Unit 9 for more about storytelling.

🎧 Listen to Flaviana, the teacher in **7E**. She has been telling the story of Little Red Riding Hood to her pupils – the extract starts at the end of the story, with Little Red Riding Hood and her grandmother safely having tea together.

The children
— know the story in their mother tongue
— have talked about the people in the story
— are going to **summarize** the story themselves
— are going write down what they remember with the help of the teacher
— will then draw a set of pictures to show what happens in the story.

---

7 E

Preparing to write about a well-known story

TEACHER: And now are they happy?
CHILDREN: They're happy.
TEACHER: And they sit at the table and eat … what?
CHILDREN: Jam and cakes.
TEACHER: Very good. Jam and cakes. Very good. OK, now we're going to write the story and to draw it. OK, now how does the story begin? Can you remember the first part of the story? Uh uh. Can you start? Who can start? Who wants to start? OK, Patricia …
PATRICIA: This is the story of Little Red Riding Hood.
TEACHER: Good, very good. And what happens to her? What happens? (*the children all talking together*)
TEACHER: Just one person. Now what's next? What comes next? Giada?
GIADA: 'Go to Granny's' Mummy says …
TEACHER: Good. Mummy says 'Go to Granny's'. Now let's write that much.

Flaviana with nine year olds.

> ## LANGUAGE FOCUS 7.3
>
> ### Story questions
>
> 🎧 Listen to the extract again and underline all the teacher's questions.
> RECORD Practise saying them after the CD with the same intonation as this teacher.
> Choose five to record on your cassette.
>
> ### Story summary
>
> ↻ Divide your page into two columns.
> In the left column, write out very simply, the basic story of Little Red Riding Hood – either in past or present simple tense – on alternate lines (leaving a space between each line).
> In the right column, opposite each line, write two questions: one that you can use to check comprehension and a second to ask children if they can add something to the line.
>
> | Red Riding Hood lived in a house with … | Who did she live with? |
> |---|---|
> | her mother. | Can you tell me what the house was like? |

7.4 Children writing freely

In this section we are going to look at some activities that can help children move to writing freely and creatively.

When children write individually about what they know or feel themselves
— they are writing to communicate with others
— they are developing self-confidence.

As a teacher you know that
— all creative effort should be praised and encouraged
— spelling and handwriting can be looked at separately
— the child's message is most important.

Writing about people

To help children write freely you can start with the kind of personal **presentation** we looked at first of all in **5E** and then in a more imaginative way in **5F** (pages 62 and 63).

Children should first of all be able to say what they are going to write.

If you look again at **5E**, you will notice how the teacher asks questions to help the children talk about themselves.

You can use a similar pattern to help children start writing.

Show the children what to do by
— drawing a simple outline of a boy or girl on the board
— letting them decide how to answer the questions. They can vote on a name or age, etc.
— writing the answers on the board, in the order the children ask them
— showing them how their answers can become a written description of the person
— showing them how to organize their answers into information sections, for example, what the person looks like/where the person lives/what the person likes to do in their free time.

When they are familiar with this writing process, let children draw a person they know or let them make up an imaginary person.

They can do this in pairs or individually.

They can work in pairs to help one another write about their person by answering questions they think are important.

TEACHING TIPS

Writing about other people

✔ When they start doing this activity on their own, children may want to keep the same questions you used on the board but you can encourage them to ask other questions and answer them. This will make their descriptions individual.

✔ If they don't put in the name of the person they are writing about, the activity can become a guessing game. Let the other pupils read the descriptions and guess who this is.

✔ Children learn from reading one another's work. You can display what children have written on the wall. They can pick the funniest/the best or guess who the person is if it is not said.

✔ If your pupils can use a computer, they can describe characters that they and the other children know, e.g. favourite cartoon characters, and use them for a computer quiz. And they can use the spell-checker.

Having fun making a book

Children enjoy making books. It gives them a feeling of achievement. They can write out the story by hand or use a computer and leave spaces for pictures to be stuck in later on.

— You can adapt the activity 'Writing about people' (page 91).

  — Let the children start by drawing a person or, for fun, an imaginary creature like a monster or a creature from outer space.

  — They can write a description as they did for 'Writing about people'.

  — Then they can write about something the person does.

My Monster

Zozie is a good monster. He lives in a box. He is yellow and furry. He's got four eyes and small feet. He sees everything.

Show children how to make a big book.
— This will give a lot of opportunity to use 'listen and make' instructions (see Unit 3).
— Let the whole class make a big storybook for another class/other classes (see Unit 9).
— They can share the work, for example, the drawings, the colouring, the writing, etc.
See Resources (pages 141–2) for more books with art and craft ideas.

Later you can divide the class into groups
— Let them write short stories for each group and draw pictures.
— If the class enjoys this activity you can let individual children write their own small books. They don't have to be very long.
— They can make up adventures for their favourite character, for example, *Zozie has a bad day, Zozie at school.*
Children can also make a book using a computer. They can
— write up their work
— use a program like 'Paint' for drawings
— print out uncoloured drawings and colour them in by hand with felt tips or markers.
When children make things for others to see, they
— have a real audience so want to write something interesting
— have a real reason to be neat and tidy, to have clear handwriting, to check their spelling and generally to present their work well
— can learn how to go over their work and improve it if they like
— bring outside knowledge into the classroom
— compare what they are doing with other children's work.

Writing to penpals

As well as writing about people they know or imagine, children love to find out about other children. Lots of children around the world are learning English. So your pupils could write to other children anywhere in the world, not just to children whose mother tongue is English.
— Writing to penpals is a very practical way to use English.
— It lets children see the real value of learning another language – to communicate and find out about other people.

— When children do this they are learning about other attitudes and ways of doing things. They are not just practising their English – they are opening their minds to the rest of the world.

Lots of teachers are interested in finding penpals for their pupils. You may be able to contact a penpal agency or contact other schools through teachers' magazines or organizations, or by using the Internet.

In the past children only wrote letters by hand. If you have access to a computer in your school, you can be in almost immediate contact with other schools and children all over the world through email.

— Children enjoy getting messages from friends on computer.
— Short messages are more like a chat.
— Regular contact helps to develop confidence and interest.
— Key pals or e-pals can be found on special Websites (see Resources, page 142). Make sure you know who your pupils are writing to.

If children become aware that English can be used to talk to or write to people in different countries, they will begin to understand why they are learning this new language.

TEACHING TIPS

Writing freely

✔ Give the children as much control as possible over what they are going to write about and how. Let them write about what they are interested in – their home – parents – interests or hobbies – friends or imaginary people and things that happen at school.

✔ Have regular days for checking mail and particular days for emailing so that children can plan and think about what they are going to write.

✔ Encourage the children to be autonomous, e.g. send them to other sources to teach them how to solve problems – dictionaries or spell-checker for spelling, information sources on the computer or other books for ideas, etc. (Of course you are there if they really need more help. You can judge this.)

✔ If children make a book as we described above, they can add other books with the same characters. Their characters can go on to have different experiences, e.g. *Zozie's holiday, Zozie's great adventure*, etc.

THINK ABOUT WRITING

— Writing is a physical skill and a language skill.
— Writing comes after other language work – so you usually have time to prepare children to start to write.
— Accept that pupils will make handwriting and/or spelling mistakes.
   — These mistakes can be corrected over time with practice.
   — They are not as important as the children's efforts to communicate.
— Praise and respect all efforts – no matter how small.
— Display as much of the pupils' writing as you can.
— Keep all their written work and reuse it in other ways if you can.
— When children are preparing to write they need
   — support and preparation before they write
   — to listen to you
   — to talk and comment.

TOPIC TALK
Food

↺ **1** Design a **mind map** (or list of topics) on the subject of food that you could use with ten to twelve year old children.

What questions might you ask them?

2 How would you prepare a pizza/a curry? What would be the **yummiest** (best) and **yuckiest** (worst) pizza toppings you could imagine?

3 Prepare to tell someone how to make your favourite dish. What are the ingredients? How do you make it?

RECORD Record yourself.

Further ideas

↺ **1** Think back over some of the speaking activities you used in class. List three. How could you use them to prepare children for writing?

2 Read Chapter 7 (pages 76-83) from **Brewster, Jean, Gail Ellis, and Denis Girard. 1992.** *The Primary English Teacher's Guide.* London: Penguin, and/or Chapter 4 from **Philips, Sarah. 1993.** *Young Learners.* Oxford: Oxford University Press.

3 Look at the writing activities from this unit, or from one of the books above, or from your coursebook. Think of how you could use two of them with your class. Plan what instructions you would give your pupils.

RECORD Record what you would say to the class when introducing the idea, and the instructions for the activities.

4 Check out the Website

http://www.startwrite.com

This site lets you write out your own text in dotted letters. The children can then trace over the letters. You can write what they say, so that their handwriting practice has a meaningful purpose as well. Think of an activity you could use it for in class.

5 Look up the Website

http://www.ks-connection.org/penpal/penpal.html

and see if there is a class or teacher you would like to contact.

NOTE
Children should only use the Internet under supervision.

8

Reading and telling stories

This unit looks at

ideas and activities on how to
- prepare to tell a story for the first time
- prepare to read a story, using pictures and familiar language
- retell stories in different ways
- get children to retell a story as a class.

Introduction

Children love stories. They
— are always eager to listen to stories
— know how stories work
— want to understand what is happening
— can enjoy hearing stories in English when they start English lessons
— enjoy looking at story books by themselves
— can reread the stories they like when they can read in English themselves.

> **REMEMBER**
> Young learners acquire language unconsciously. The activities you do in class should help this kind of acquisition. Stories are the most valuable resource you have. They offer children a world of supported meaning that they can relate to. Later on you can use stories to help children practise listening, speaking, reading, and writing.

The value of stories

Read the paragraphs below. From each paragraph, decide which are the four most important reasons for using stories in your classes.

The educational value of stories

Stories
— help children relate new things to what they know already
— help children to look at real life from different viewpoints and imagine what it feels like to be someone else
— can introduce the child to other cultures and attitudes
— let children share their experiences with the group – everyone listens and feels sad or happy
— can link to other subjects the child is learning about in school
— help children develop their thinking skills
— are interesting and enjoyable, and can be fun.

Stories for language teaching

Stories
— can be told with pictures and **gestures** to help children understand
— help children enjoy learning English
— introduce new language in **context**
— help children **revise** language they are familiar with
— help children become **aware** of the structures of the language
— help children **acquire intonation** and pronunciation by listening
— can help bring English into other subjects
— can lead on to lots of activities using listening, speaking, reading, and writing.

Stories are first of all for enjoyment. Children need to understand something about the story (not every word, but the main **gist** or story line) if they are going to enjoy it. Pictures and gestures help a lot, but your **intonation** and the way you tell it or read it are very important.

> **REMEMBER**
> There is a difference between telling and reading a story.
> One of the most important differences is your intonation pattern.
>
> 1 When you tell a story you
>   — speak **spontaneously**
>   — use natural **intonation** to help make the story seem real
>   — are looking at the children and you can see if they understand
>   — can use your face and body to make **gestures**
>   — practise first and have some support, e.g. notes on cards
>   — don't need to worry if you make mistakes (children are unlikely to notice).
>
> 2 When you read a story you can
>   — repeat and rephrase in a natural way
>   — stop and talk to the children about what is happening
>   — stop and show pictures and talk about them
>   — sometimes talk to individuals about an aspect of the story.

8A

Telling a story after preparation

TEACHER: I'm going to tell you a story about two animals. Look. The animals are …
(*The teacher puts up the two pictures on the blackboard and points as she speaks.*)

TEACHER AND CHILDREN: (*together*) A bird and …

TEACHER: … And an elephant.

CHILDREN: (*All shout*) A fox!

TEACHER: No … It's an elephant!

CHILDREN: … a fox!

TEACHER: It's a fox. I'm going to tell you a story about a bird and a fox.
(*As the teacher tells the story, she points to the cards.*)

TEACHER: A fox saw a bird eating some cheese.
(*The teacher shows the children the pretend piece of cheese.*)
    And the fox said, 'Hey you, give me your cheese. I like cheese and I'm really hungry.'
    The bird said, 'No, you can't have my cheese.'
    And the fox said, 'Can you fly, bird?'
    And the bird said 'Yes I can fly.'
    'So fly down here to me and give me your cheese.'
    And the bird said, 'Look I can fly but you can't have my cheese.'
    And the fox said, 'Can you sing, bird?'
    And the bird said, 'Yes, I can sing. Listen to my song'
    And the bird …
(*Here the teacher gestures with her hand to show that the bird opens his mouth and that cheese falls to the ground.*)
    … and says 'Oh no, my cheese!'
    And the fox said, 'Ha, ha, ha … Now I've got your cheese. It's my favourite … mmmm.'

Pura with nine to ten year olds.

8.1 Telling a new story

⊶ How do you prepare yourself to tell children a story for the first time? List three things you might do so that you tell it well.
    — Look back at the classroom extracts **4B**, **4C**, and **4D** (pages 47 and 48). The teacher was revising words for animals the children knew and introducing some new words to her class, especially for this story.

🎧 — Now listen to the teacher in **8A** telling the story.
    — Notice how she catches the pupils' attention by saying the fox was an elephant!
    — The teacher tells this story using picture flashcards and her own actions. The language is basic and clear. As you listen, imagine you are telling it.
    — What actions or **gestures** would you use?
    — Would you use different voices for the fox and the bird?

LANGUAGE FOCUS 8.1

Intonation and actions

1 Listen to the CD again, and this time try to tell the story along with the teacher, with the same intonation and stress. Try this a couple of times.

2 Listen again, doing the same thing, but this time doing the actions that you think would help children's enjoyment of the story.

3 Think of a class you know. What changes might you make to this story for them?

RECORD Record yourself telling the same story, as if for your own class.

Story questions and prompts

a *Who...?* **questions**

Practise asking these questions until you can say them fast. Can you imagine the answers you might get? The children can say simply *The bird* or *The fox*.

	was eating the cheese (at the begining of the story)?
	saw the bird eating the cheese?
	wanted the cheese?
Who	asked the bird some questions?
	sang a beautiful song?
	dropped the cheese?
	ate the cheese in the end?

b *What...?* **questions**

Add some more short answers to the table, then practise all six questions, giving possible answers.

	was the bird eating?	He asked him to sing a song.
	was the fox thinking?	...
What	did the fox ask first?	...
	did he do then?	He flew away to another wood.
	do you think they both did next?	...
	do you think will happen next?	...

c *How/Why do you think...?* **questions**

Read the tables. Think what the answers would be and then practise asking and answering these questions.

Why do you think he asked the bird to sing?	because he liked listening to birds singing?
	to make him open his mouth wide?
	to make him drop the cheese?

How do you think	the bird felt, at first?	happy? pleased? sad?
	he felt at the end?	hungry? jealous?
	the fox felt, at first?	proud? cross? angry?
	at the end?	a bit silly? stupid?

RECORD Choose some questions from each table to record on your cassette. Grade them before you record – i.e. start with the ones that will be easiest for your children, and end with the most difficult.

Write down the simplest answers that children might give to each question; practise rephrasing these answers, then building on them.

Telling and performing a story with very young learners

Using body language, **gestures**, and actions is very important to all learners, but especially to very young learners. When children act and perform a story they quickly become familiar with the language you use. This is how one teacher told a story with her class.

The children already know Spot the dog from storybooks (see Resources, page 142).

The children stand in a circle and copy the teacher while she is telling the story.

The teacher says	The teacher and children
Spot is looking for baby animals	— start looking all around the classroom
miaou, miaou	— all make a cat sound
Who's that?	— ask the question with a hand gesture
a cat…	— pretend to be a cat
no baby animals here	— wave their finger to say 'no' with a sad face

The teacher goes on telling the story, asking children to introduce other animals.

At the end of the story Spot finds some baby animals.

The teacher says	The teacher and children
Oh look, piglets – hurray!!	— point and jump up and down
Spot is very happy now.	— clap their hands

By telling the story this way the teacher is involving the children and helping them connect the language they are hearing with what they are doing – and there is no need for pictures. (Many thanks to Silvana Rampone for this story idea.)

Telling a story

✔ Some teachers arrange their class differently for story time, like the teacher in **2G** (page 25) who arranged her class to learn a new song.

✔ When you tell a new story to children who are just beginning to learn English you can
  — tell the bare story line in English using lots of dialogue, actions, gestures, and sound effects for animals and machines
  — let the children ask you questions in their mother tongue and show them again with actions, gestures, and pictures what you mean
  — let the children's questions show you what you have to make clearer.
✔ When telling a story for the first time to any group of children
  — use actions, gestures, pictures or other support material
  — let the children **predict** what they think will happen next (it doesn't matter if they predict in their mother tongue – accept their contribution and **recast** it in English.)
  — change, leave out bits, and add to a story to make it more suitable for your class
  — practise repeating phrases and adding questions for the children
  — practise using your voice for characters – speak loudly, softly, slowly, high-pitch or low-pitch – according to the character
  — involve the children as much as possible
  — speak to them and look at them when you are telling the story.

If, after all this, there is something important that children do not understand, go over it again and explain the problem in their mother tongue and then say it again in English.

8.2 Reading a story to very young learners

When you tell a story to children you can help them understand by
— using a book with pictures
— showing them real things that are talked about in the story
— miming what happens in the story to help children understand meaning
— make the sounds for things in the story, for example, *animals*, *trains*
— repeating **key words** and **phrases**
— asking and answering questions about the story.

Listening to a story and looking at the pictures

Now you are going to hear a teacher, Susan, with very young learners (see also **1L**, page 18).

They are reading a story together called *Elmer* (see Resources, page 142). Elmer is different from all the other elephants because he is brightly coloured – all the colours of the rainbow. Here is the text that Susan is reading from.

As he walked in the jungle Elmer met all the animals. They always said 'Good morning Elmer.'

Each time Elmer smiled and said: 'Good morning.'

After a long walk, Elmer found what he was looking for – a large bush – a large bush covered with berries.

Elmer caught hold of the bush and shook it and shook it so that the berries fell on the ground.

(From *Elmer* by David McKee)

---

8 B

Listening to a story and looking at pictures

TEACHER: And Elmer, as he walked in the jungle, Elmer met all the animals and they always said, 'Good morning, Elmer.'

And each time Elmer smiled and said …

What did Elmer say? Sh … sh … sh He said … he said 'Good morning.' What did Elmer say?

ALL THE CHILDREN: Good morning.

TEACHER: After a long walk, Elmer found what he was looking for. A very big bush.

A large bush covered with elephant berries.

What colour are elephant berries? What colour?

Grey. They're grey. Elephant coloured berries. Grey berries.

See Elmer. He caught hold of the bush and shook it and shook it.

ONE CHILD REPEATS: Shook it.

TEACHER: And all the berries fell on the ground. See him he's shaking, shaking the bush. See them … see them … see all the berries.

ONE CHILD REPEATS: See them.

Susan with six year olds.

Listen to **8B** and notice the difference between the written story and the way the teacher tells it.

These very young children naturally
— repeat the phrases Susan uses
— talk a lot in their mother tongue about what they can see in the pictures.

8 C

Talking about what is happening

TEACHER: On the way, he passed the
   other animals again. See, he's
   going by...
      Each one said. Listen to what they
   said, 'Good morning elephant.'
   What did they say?

CHILDREN: Good morning, elephant.

TEACHER: Did they know it was Elmer?
   Do they know Elmer?

CHILDREN: No.

TEACHER: Elmer smiled and said,
   'Good morning.'
   What did he say?

CHILDREN: Good morning.

TEACHER: And he was pleased that he
   wasn't recognized. They didn't
   recognize him.
      Look at all the elephants...
   (*The children look at the pictures and
   talk in their mother tongue.*)

TEACHER: When Elmer rejoined all the
   elephants...
   (*One child interrupts and says in his
   mother tongue that all the elephants
   together look like an army and another
   child says they are not smiling.*)

TEACHER: Yes it looks like an army of
   elephants, doesn't it? All grey
   elephants. Yes. And not smiling...

CHILD: Purple... purple.

TEACHER: Well nearly grey. They were all
   standing quietly. See them standing
   quietly. You know 'be quiet'...
   Did they see him?

CHILDREN: No.

TEACHER: Did he see him?

CHILDREN: No.

TEACHER: Are they smiling? Are they
   happy? Not happy. What are they?
   They are very quiet.

CHILD: Very, very quiet.

TEACHER: And are they happy?

CHILDREN: No.

TEACHER: Not smiling. Not happy.

Susan with six year olds.

> LANGUAGE FOCUS 8.2a
>
> ## Story questions and prompts
>
> 1 How many questions and **prompts** does this teacher use in **8B**? Can you
>   find five or six?
>
>   Listen for them on the CD, then say them with the teacher.
>
> 2 Read the table. Make five sensible questions, and suggest one obviously
>   silly answer and one correct answer for each one.
>
> RECORD   Record these on your cassette, for example,
>   — *What did Elmer shake? His head? (No!) The bush? (Yes!)*
>
> | Who did | | meet in the jungle? |
> |------------|-------|----------------------------|
> | | Elmer | always say to them? |
> | What did | | find, after his long walk? |
> | | he | shake? |
> | What might | | do next, do you think? |

Moving away from the text

Later in **8C** the teacher uses the children's familiarity with colours to
involve them more in the text. At this point, Elmer has been rolling in the
berries hoping that the berry juice will make him grey. The teacher asks
questions that fit the context of the story.
— *He's covered himself in berry juice. Grey. Will he be yellow? Will he be
   purple? Will he be grey?*
As the teacher asks about all the colours the children know, she increases
the children's interest in the story.

Talking about what is happening

In children's stories there is often repetition of the same situation.
Children enjoy repeating the same kind of language that was used in
other parts of the story.

Read the extract **8C** and put an arrow (→) by each line where these five
things happen:
a The teacher uses a checking question to make sure the children
   understand what is happening.
b The children repeat things the teacher has said.
c The teacher reminds children of the language they already know.
d The teacher recasts in English what the children comment on either
   in English or in their mother tongue.
e The teacher repeats the chunks of language she wants the children
   to become familiar with.

Listen twice to **8C**. The second time say the teacher's part along with
the teacher.
At the end of this story the children talk to their teacher about the
colours they can see and the colours they like.

LANGUAGE FOCUS 8.2b

Telling and talking

↻ Read **8C** again.

Underline under all the parts the teacher is actually reading from the book, telling the story.

🎧 Check by listening again to the CD.

Then study the parts where she talks about the book. She uses instructions questions for different purposes. Listen and repeat all these, talking along with the teacher, for example, *see, he's going to …*

🎧 Pronunciation point

Sounds /t/, /d/, and /ɪd/

⟿ Say these eight words and group them according to the pronunciation of their *-ed* endings. Do they end in /t/ or /d/ or /ɪd/?

passed	*pleased*	*recognized*	*rejoined*
smiled	*walked*	*covered*	*decorated*

Extension ideas

At the end of the story, the elephants celebrate 'Elmer's Day'.
— Make an Elmer's Day poster.
— Give out outline drawings of elephants and let the children colour them in.
— Get the children to choose **labels** of **phrases** from the book as reading cards – they can add them to the poster to remind them of what was said, e.g.

He shouted BOOO!
On one day a year they decorate themselves and parade.

TEACHING TIPS

Reading a story

✔ Read the story several times before you use it in class.
✔ Practise reading and telling the story aloud.
✔ Record yourself, then play it back, and listen to it.
✔ Prepare
— the questions you are going to ask the children – about the pictures and about the story
— how to rephrase phrases in the story
— the comments you could make about the pictures.

✔ Keep all the stories you read in your reading corner and encourage children to look at them again.
✔ When children can read, set them reading tasks, e.g.
How many times did Elmer say 'Good morning?' or *Put this set of reading cards in the right order.*

8.3 Ways to retell a story

When children have heard a story once, you can tell it again. Each time
you retell a story, children
— will become more familiar with the language of the story
— will be able to participate more
— will be able to participate in different ways.

When the children are listening, you can
— stop telling the story and see if the children can remember what
  happens next
— put up some pictures of scenes from the story. Ask children to point to
  the picture of what or who you are telling them about.
— ask the class to stand up and mime all the actions as they happen
— divide the class up so that each group can pretend to be one of the
  main characters. Each group becomes that character and only mimes
  the actions he/she does.
— act out the story as you tell it, and later get some children to take parts,
  come out to the front, and act with you
— let the children sit in groups. Give a set of pictures from the story to
  each group. As you tell the story ask the groups to put the pictures into
  the right sequence.
— ask the children to listen carefully, then make some deliberate
  mistakes/changes, e.g. *One day a fox saw a bird eating a hamburger.*
— use **Cuisenaire rods** for the characters and places in the story and ask
  the children to say what is happening.

Cuisenaire rods

If the children can read, you can
— give out cards with the key words and phrases from the story written
  on them. Ask each child to hold up their word when they hear it

wolf   *house made of straw*   *house made of brick*   *little pig*   *house made of wood*   *huff and puff*

— write out the story in sentences on cards and ask groups of children to put them in the right sequence after you have told the story again.

LANGUAGE FOCUS 8.3

Instructions when retelling a story

↻ Read the ideas in this section again. Choose four different ways you might retell a story.

RECORD Write and record four different sets of instructions, with examples, telling the children what to do while you are telling the story in this way.

I'm going to read you the same story again, only this time I want you to stand up and mime all the actions as you hear me read about them. So you listen. Then mime what they do, OK? Like this – if I read 'her mother gave her the basket' you do – what?

8.4 Retelling a story as a class

If you use stories frequently, the children will know a lot of stories. Children enjoy retelling a story with you.

Retelling from memory

🎧 Listen to the teacher in 8D getting the children to retell the story of *The Three Little Pigs*. The children remember the story – but not some of the language.

Notice how the teacher accepts what they say, using positive words like 'OK', and does not correct the structures because the children are getting the meaning across very well.

— She often rephrases and recasts what they are trying to say, adding the right words.
— She does not interfere – but helps quickly by giving them the language they need.
— She builds on their responses, adding detail.

8 D

Retelling *The Three Little Pigs*

TEACHER: OK, so what is the first thing that happens in *The Three Little Pigs*, John?

JOHN: Once a pig made a house and a fox ... and the fox ... blew it ...

TEACHER: Blew it ... blew it down. OK, that's right. OK, the first pig made his house with? What did he build it with? What did he build that house with?

JOHN: Grass.

TEACHER: Yeah. Grass. Straw. He built it out of grass. That's right. And who blew it down?

JOHN: A fox ...

TEACHER: A fox? A wolf.

CHILDREN: Yes. Yes. A wolf.

TEACHER: That's right and the second pig ...

CHILD: The little pig going to his brother's house.

TEACHER: And what did that little pig make his house out of?

CHILD: A wooden house.

TEACHER: OK, a house made out of?

CHILDREN: Wood.

TEACHER: That's right. Yes. Wood. Sticks. Branches from the tree. He built his house out of sticks.

Candace with ten to eleven year olds (re-recorded by Alan).

8 E

Preparing for a new story

TEACHER: Now this story is called 'The Real Story of the Three Little Pigs.' And the wolf is telling the story. So, what do you think the wolf is going to say?

CHILD: Eat the three little pigs.

TEACHER: So he's going to say, 'Yes I'm very bad. I ate the three little pigs.' So what else do you think he's going to say?

CHILD: He's going to say ... I went to the pig's house and ... and say please ... open the door and not open and ...

TEACHER: So he's going to say 'I said please open the door and they said no they were so rude. Right. They were so rude.' OK and ... Yes, Narn?

NARN: He's changing his clothes and saying 'I'm your mum.'
(*The children all know the story of Little Red Riding Hood and they all laugh.*)

TEACHER: So, 'I'm your mum'. That sounds like *Little Red Riding Hood*.

Katherine with ten to eleven year olds (re-recorded by Alan).

Retelling from a different point of view

The children in **8D** were retelling the story because they are going to read another story in **8E**. This is also about the three little pigs – but it is the wolf's story. The teacher
— **revises** the original story
— asks the children to predict what they think the wolf will say when he tells his version of the story.

Listen to **8E** and notice
— how the teacher listens as the children answer – and then rephrases and recasts what they say
— how the children can connect different stories and be very inventive.

As we can see in **8E**, children are able to use the stories they know to express more than just the story.
— The language in stories is supported by **context**.
— This helps children understand.
— When they understand they become more interested and more confident.
— And confidence helps them to take chances with language and try to communicate.

LANGUAGE FOCUS 8.4

Stress on key words

Read the teacher's part of **8E** and mark the words you think are the **key words**, the words that must be **stressed**. You should find around 13 or 14.

Then listen to the CD and check to see if those words are stressed. There may be some other words stressed too. Think about why these words are stressed.

Finally repeat the teacher's part, then choose one section (about five lines) to record on your cassette.

TEACHING TIPS

Retelling stories

✔ Keep all pictures with the story in a story pack.
   — Take these out before you retell the story.
   — The pictures will help children remember the English words.

✔ Encourage the children to do the telling.

✔ Do not interrupt while they are trying to communicate.

Story time

NOTE
In this unit, Story Time will replace Topic Talk and Further Ideas.

Think of two stories suitable for a class you teach, one you can tell, and one you can read. Then follow these steps, to prepare each story for your class.

1 Plan how you would introduce the class to each story, and how you would prepare for it.

2 Plan what pictures or other visual aids you would use, and how and when you would use them. What might you say about each picture to the children? Suggest two things for each picture.

3 Write a list of questions you might ask for each page or part of the story (some easy ones and some more open-ended ones.) For each question, think of two possible answers that children may give.

4 Plan two ways of retelling each story, asking children to do something different each time, to make it fun for them. Work out what instructions you would need to give.

RECORD 5 Find a person/some people you can tell your story to, as a rehearsal for your lesson. Record yourself telling the story to this person, talking about it and asking questions. Then record yourself retelling it to the same people in a different way.

Read Chapter 1 from **Wright, Andrew. 1995.** *Storytelling with Children*. Oxford: Oxford University Press.

9

Story activities

This unit looks at

- how activities from Units 2–7 can be adapted for use with stories
- more follow-up ideas and activities that you can use with stories
- how stories provide a meaningful context for children when they are acquiring a language.

Introduction

We can use stories to give children more practice at listening, speaking, reading, and writing, as well as to **stimulate** their imagination and creativity. Some examples follow.

1 Listening

'Listen and do' – the children act like a character in a story, for example, Red Riding Hood walking in the forest, or the wolf, etc.

'Listen and perform' – they act out a story, such as *The Fox and the Cheese*.

'Listen and identify' – they point to the picture in a story.

'Listen and respond' – they listen and clap if the teacher makes a mistake in the story, for example, *Once upon a time there was a little girl called Little Blue Riding Hood* …

'Listen and colour' – they follow instructions to colour a story poster.

'Listen and draw' – they draw three things Red Riding Hood had in her basket.

'Listen and make' – they trace and cut out a face mask of a character.

2 Speaking

Children can get valuable speaking practice through:

— saying rhymes and singing songs. Some books have rhymes about stories, or you can make up a simple question-and-answer rhyme about the story. Or use a rhyme pattern that you know, such as:

> *This is the way she walks through the wood*
> *walks through the wood*
> *walks through the wood*
> *This is the way she walks through the wood*
> *On a lovely summer morning*

— playing vocabulary games. Make picture cards for matching games: collect pairs or classifying sets, for example, the pig and the wolf from *The Three Little Pigs*.

— practising new sounds. Let them play 'I spy' with items from the story, in *Little Red Riding Hood: I spy with my little eye something beginning with 'b'.*

— starting to speak freely. Elicit personal talk, for example, *you are the fox – talk about yourself: I am Mr Fox. I live in the forest. I have three brothers. I like cheese!*

— playing speaking games, led by you, for example, they pass the ball and answer questions about the story, such as: *What did the animals always say to Elmer?*

— speaking in groups. They can prepare a guessing game for the class, together, for example, *We live in three little houses. One is made of straw, one is made of sticks, and one is made of brick. Who are we?*

3 Reading

When children are learning to read, you can help them with these techniques:
— Look and say – they point to words as you tell the story, labelling a story poster
— Phonics – they group all the words in the story with the same sound, for example, *hood, house*
— Speaking to reading – helping sound and word recognition. You use pictures of the new words in the story and giving the children the syllable beats – two for *basket/forest*, etc.
— Speaking to reading – helping children to recognize phrases and make phrases from single words, for example,
   the big bad wolf/covered with elephant berries
— The alphabet – practising the names of the letters and drawing attention to the letters in stories
— Reading independently – asking the children to find information, for example,
   What did the elephants say when Elmer shouted 'Boo'?

4 Writing

These activities will help children with starting to write and with spelling:
— Classifying and copying selected words and phrases from story books:
   nature words, action words/phrases: he walked and walked …
— Labelling pictures from stories, for example,
   Here are the three little pigs outside their house …
— Finishing comments, such as
   The bird felt angry because the fox …
— Gap-filling from a story, for example,
   She put the … and cakes in her basket.

9.1 Things to do after retelling a story

Adapting a story

If you change the plot of the story a little bit, but keep the characters and setting similar, you can use familiar words and phrases but still hold the children's interest because of the new story line.

This is what the teacher in **9A**, Juan, does. (You have already heard Juan in **1E, 1J, 2E**, and **3C**). Juan's story is adapted from another story about a very hungry caterpillar.

The children are very excited because they have been playing a game and now they have to be quiet and listen. They have heard the story before and know that they can join in.

9 A

Retelling a story the children know

TEACHER: OK, OK, now listen … listen.

It's time to tell a story, OK, it's time to tell a story, it's time to tell a story, OK, a story, a story in silence, OK, in silence, we must be silent, OK … sh … OK … we'll sit on the floor. In silence we must be. OK.

This story … this is the story of the green caterpillar. OK. Now in silence we must be. OK … so … sh … OK.

This is the story of Mr Caterpillar. Sh … OK, OK. Once upon a time there was a green caterpillar. He was always hungry. One day he met a banana. 'Mmmm mmmm,' he said, 'I'm very hungry.'

So he ate it. But surprise, surprise. His head became yellow. And he walked and he walked.

(*The teacher gestures to all the children to join in.*)

CHILDREN: And he walked and he walked …

Juan with seven to eight year olds.

Listen to Juan's story in **9A** and think about what activities you could do with this class by using this story.

This caterpillar walks on and meets lots of things that he eats and drinks. He changes colour according to what he eats. The children join in with the storytelling and gain a lot of speaking practice.

A 'make and do' activity based on the story

Here is a follow-up activity that another teacher used. He
— gave the children a plain drawing of the caterpillar
— let each child choose seven types of food or drink for their caterpillar
— let the children colour all the caterpillars. The caterpillars were the same colour as the food and drink.
— asked some children to describe their caterpillars to the class
— put all the new caterpillar drawings on the wall as a display. They were all different colours.

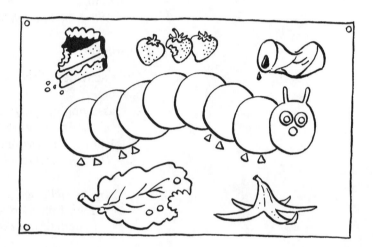

While the children coloured their drawing the teacher repeated parts of the story. He also went round the class and talked to individual children about what they were doing. (*Why has your caterpillar gone green? Because …?*)

So the children listened and spoke about the colours and food and drink that they were familiar with.

You could also ask children to write the names of the things their caterpillar ate and the colours that he became.

LANGUAGE FOCUS 9.1

Reading with feeling

Listen to Juan beginning the story in **9A**, and try to imitate the way he tells the story. Notice especially the way he says these three phrases:

He was always hungry   Mmmm mmmm   but surprise, surprise

Then read it out loud from the transcript. Record yourself and see how similar your intonation is.

Starting a feedback chat

Here are some things you can say to children who are working on their own, colouring, writing, or drawing. The context for this table is the caterpillar story.

Choose a story you might do this activity with. This table is about the caterpillar story. Change some of the words, comments, and questions in the tables to suit your story. Your aim is to encourage individual children to have a short conversation or chat with you about their work.

That's a	very nice	caterpillar!	Can you tell me more about it?
	lovely	picture!	Why did you do that bit yellow?
	wonderful		How many things has he eaten?
	fantastic		Wow, has he eaten all those things? or only some?
That's	really good	colouring	What things does he like best?
	pretty good	writing	My goodness – he's got a lot of legs! Can he walk very fast?
	very neat	drawing	So now, what are you going to draw/write/colour next?

RECORD Practise four or five feedback examples, then record them.

Extension ideas

Get children to tell the story from another point of view. What would the wolf say in *The Three Little Pigs*? (See Resources, page 142, for the published version.)

TEACHING TIPS

Working on activities about a story

✔ As you go round the class,
  — encourage children to talk to you about what they are doing or have done
  — ask questions with one- or two-word answers, as well as questions which make children talk more

  — look at what they have done and talk about it, even if they won't understand everything you say
  — give your shy pupils more chance to talk to you individually than you give confident students (who talk in class anyway!)

✔ You can use the same kind of feedback chat when you go round the class to check children's homework.

---

9 B

Starting a story and letting the children continue

TEACHER: Now I will tell you a story. Now please listen to me carefully and try to memorize the story. Now close your eyes. Close your eyes. Everybody. There is a wonderful zoo in Kitakyushu. You are in the zoo. This zoo is very nice, but it's a funny zoo. It's a little bit unusual. (*Teacher also explains about this unusual zoo in her mother tongue.*)

Let's walk around in the zoo. Now try to remember what I tell you. OK. Now some blue birds are singing and some pink birds are playing tennis. (*Some pupils laugh.*)

TEACHER: A lion is eating a hamburger. A tiger is reading a book and a sheep is dancing. OK. (*Some pupils laugh.*)

TEACHER: OK, open your eyes. Now, I would like to check your memory. (*later in the same class*)

TEACHER: OK, very good, you remembered very well. Now boys and girls, can you make another funny story about this zoo? (*Some pupils answer in their mother tongue.*)

MATSUDA: A dog is …

TEACHER: Yes. What is the dog doing?

MATSUDA: A dog is playing violin.

TEACHER: A dog is playing the violin. Good. Any more?

TEACHER: No? OK, you have … oh yeah! Sagisaka-kun.

SAGISAKA: A snake is riding a bicycle.

TEACHER: A snake is riding a bicycle!

CHILDREN: A bicycle.

Fumiko with ten year olds.

9.2 Getting children to add to a story

In **9B** you are going to listen to another teacher, Fumiko. You have listened to Fumiko's class before, in **5D**. They were looking for four differences in their pictures. The differences were all about what people were doing.

The short story that Fumiko now tells her class is also about actions. She tells her pupils a story about a strange zoo. In this zoo the animals do unusual things. The story allows the children to revise a grammatical structure in a fun way. Notice how Fumiko starts the story and then lets the children continue.

Before the extract in **9B**, the pupils had been talking about what people are doing in pictures.

Now they are being creative and using what they know to communicate new ideas.

After this, they could each write their own stories about the zoo.

LANGUAGE FOCUS 9.2

From speaking to story writing

To help your class write their own story about the strange zoo, you might use tables such as these – see boxes 1–4.

BOX 1	
Last week-end	my family and I went to the zoo.
Last week	
Last Sunday	my friends and I went to the park.
Last holidays	

BOX 2	
Near the entrance,	we saw a tiger reading a book.
Further on,	we heard a monkey singing.
Then,	there was a snake riding a bicycle.
Round the corner,	there were some white deer dancing.
In one cage,	a panda was swimming in a pond.
Near the lake,	
Near the exit	

BOX 3

It was all very funny/interesting/strange/silly.
It was great fun and very entertaining.

BOX 4

We had a great/wonderful day out.
We got home and told everyone all about it.
But nobody believed us! Not even my Dad/Grandmother!
We hope to go back again soon.

➲ Choose a set of sentences from the boxes that could make a story.
Read them out loud to the class, pointing to the phrases as you
read them.
Read slowly, as if the children were reading along with you.
Read one sentence from Box 1, and three or four from Box 2.
End your story with two or three sentences from Boxes 3 and 4.
Practise reading your sample story out loud with lots of expression.

RECORD Record one **version** of the story on your cassette.

➲ Think of a story that you could use for an activity like this – a story familiar
to one of your classes. Make up your own set of boxes for this story that
your class could read from and then write their own story from.

🎧 Pronunciation point

Sound /s/. Clusters /st/, /sn/, /sl/, /str/

o┉ Say these words and decide how you would group them. You can put them
into five groups.

surprise	*slap*	*story*	*stamp*
snap	*supermarket*	*stand*	*step*
sneeze	*start*	*strawberries*	*sleep*

Practise saying these clusters smoothly. The letter *s* blends with the next
consonant sound.

9.3 Making up a story

In the Resources section (page 142) there is a list of published story books
that teachers have recommended. But you can also make up a story of
your own for your class. If you make up a story you can
— make it more personal and local – about people/animals/places the
children know well
— include language the children are familiar with
— include topics they are learning about
— use materials you have already used but in a different way, for
example, photos or pictures of animals.
— prepare it so that the children can do follow-up activities such as
colouring or mime.

➲ Here is a sample story made up for a class. Read it silently, imagining in
your head the actions, the gestures, and the intonation and expression
you would use to get the meaning across. Read it again and underline
any phrases that you might use at other times in class, or that your
children might be familiar with.

RECORD Finally read it out loud to someone, and record it on your teaching
cassette, so that you can use it in class.

Alva and the robin

Alva is a little girl.
She lives in a house with a lovely garden.
She likes talking and singing and playing with
    her friends.
But today her friends are away with their families.
She is on her own and feels very sad.
She walks out into the garden – all by herself.
She sees a robin in a tree.
'Hello robin,' says Alva. 'How are you today?'
'Oh, I'm fine. How are you?' says the robin.
'Oh,' says Alva, 'you can speak.'
'Yes,' says the robin, 'and I can sing too.'
'Oh,' says Alva, 'what else can you do?'
'Well, I can fly, of course,' says the robin.
'Oh,' says Alva, 'I can't fly. I wish I could fly. I want
    to visit my friends.'
'Would you like to meet some of my friends?' says
    the robin. 'They are here in the garden.'
Alva looks around. 'I don't see anyone.'
'Oh, you have to look carefully,' says the robin.
    'Look over there, there's a ladybird.'
'Where?' says Alva.
'Over there,' says the robin, 'under the big
    green leaf.'
And Alva walks over and picks up the leaf and
    there's the ladybird.

'Oh, I can see you, ladybird,' says Alva. 'Good
    morning, ladybird.'
'She's in a hurry,' says the robin.
'And here is a butterfly,' says the robin.
'Where?' says Alva.
'Over there,' says the robin, 'in those flowers.'
 And Alva walks over and looks in the flowers.
'Can you see all his colours?' says the robin.
    'There's red and yellow and blue and purple
    and orange and brown.'
'Oh, I can see you, butterfly,' says Alva. 'Good
    morning, butterfly.'
'And now,' says the robin, 'here are my other
    friends.'
'Where?' says Alva.
'Over there,' says the robin, 'on top of the tree.'
 And Alva walks over and looks in the tree and
    there are lots of birds.
'Oh, I can see you all,' says Alva. 'Good morning,
    birds.'
'Now,' says the robin, 'you know all my friends.'
'Thank you, robin,' says Alva. 'I am having a nice
    time.'

Extension ideas

Adapt this story by
— using local birds, insects, or small animals your pupils are
   familiar with
— putting in other samples of positions these creatures are found in, for
   example, *under a stone, on a wall, behind a bush.*

Do a project on Alva and her new friends. Make a wall display based on
the natural environment in your area. Let the children
— suggest what creatures to have in the display
— draw or make a collage of each creature where it is usually found, for
   example, *a butterfly on a flower, an insect on a stone*
— use labels if they are starting to read.
You can use this kind of **cross-curricular** activity as part of an English
lesson and in your natural science lessons. Children learn in this way
that all language is about meaning.

LANGUAGE FOCUS 9.3

Story structure

The story of Alva and the robin shows one very common structure for
a story.
— **Situation**
   Who Alva is and what she likes (lines 1–3).
— **Problem**
   Alva is on her own as her friends are away (lines 4–6).
— **Solution**
   She talks to the robin who introduces her to his friends (line 7 to the
   last line).
— **Evaluation**
   Alva comments on her experience (last line).
Traditional stories often follow this pattern. They usually start with a
character and a situation, then they introduce the problem, for example,
Goldilocks was very hungry.
   Then there are one or more solutions, for example, *Goldilocks found the
bears' house and ate the porridge.*
   And the story usually ends with a positive comment, for example, *They
all lived happily ever after.*

↻ Think of a story that follows this pattern and think how you would tell it to
a class.

RECORD   Practise reading it out loud, then record yourself reading it.

9.4 Using stories for project work

Children use language in a natural and spontaneous way when they are active.
Projects
— help co-operation between children
— can be organized so that all skills are practised while you are planning and preparing it together.

> **REMEMBER**
> You do a language project to
> — bring together all the language work you have been doing in class
> — build on and extend what your pupils already know
> — allow children to work together and co-operate
> — give everyone in the class a chance to contribute
> — **achieve** something worthwhile that other people can see and that everyone can be proud of.

A favourite story project

When children have read a few stories, you could do a story project.
Talk to the children about
— why you are doing it (they can show how much English they know)
— what they want to make or do:
   a wall display, a big book, a performance, a puppet show based on the story
— what they want to put in it:
   characters, events from the story
— how they want to do it,
   in groups, the whole class together
— who will come to see it:
   their parents, other classes, other teachers
— where they will display it or perform it when it is finished:
   in their classroom, in a another part of the school.

Make a plan together and decide when you want to finish. Decide how often you are going to work on the project:
   once a week.
— Make sure that everyone is clear about what they have to do and what they have to achieve:
   draw and colour a picture of a story character and be able to say something about this character.
— Plan what the group/s have to do each day up to the final day.
— Allow starting and finishing time to take out and put away all the materials the children will use.

Decide how many stories are going to be in the project, for example, one/two favourite stories. This is the children's choice and also depends on
— the number of children in the class
— how much work they are going to do on each story.

Make sure the children know it is their project and their work.
— You have to help with organization.
— You might be able to get the art teacher to co-operate with the drawing/painting that is needed.

Use English all the time while you are working on the project (but explain quickly in the children's mother tongue anything that they find really difficult).

Here are two sample plans for a project on favourite stories. But first let the children pick their favourite story.

For a wall display children could produce
— drawings of characters
— coloured/painted backgrounds
— collages – pictures made from coloured paper and other materials
— labels – naming all the people and places in the story
— cards saying what they like and why.
They could
— invite their families and other classes to see the display
— write invitations or notices in English
— decide how they are going to show the display, e.g.
    who will be at the door to tell people where to start
    who will show each part
    what each person will say and do on the presentation day.

For a performance, children could
— decide how to perform, some could read parts of the story while others could mime
— take parts and plan what to say; to do this you could help them write out what they want to say and they could rehearse like actors
— make the story into a musical by adding songs on the themes
— make masks for their parts – with similar masks several children can act as one character
— make puppets for each part
— bring in or make simple props and/or costumes
— prepare and draw invitations for their families and other classes
— make a poster advertising their performance
— choose music to go with the story
— hold rehearsals.

9.5 Correction and project work

If children are going to perform in public, or write for an outside audience, it is important that what they say or write is well-organized, tidy, and as **accurate** as possible. This will make a good impression on the audience.

You will need to act as their language adviser
1 Find out what meanings they want to express.
2 Suggest new words and phrases that help them express these meanings.
Keep some dictionaries in the classroom while you do projects, so that children can check their own spellings and look up useful words and phrases.

Be prepared to
— encourage children to be creative and to use their imagination
— help them improve and correct their speaking or writing.

At the preparation stage – to prepare the final draft
— correct the project
— explain to the children that this is correction time
— let them do as much correction as they can.

The children
— know they are performing or displaying to a wider audience
— are likely to take more notice of corrections in these circumstances
— should be involved in as much of the correcting process as possible.

A project should also
— encourage co-operation
— give children more confidence
— give you the opportunity to praise children's efforts
— give children a chance to show what they can do apart from English.
So be realistic!

> **REMEMBER**
> — You will not be able to correct all their mistakes.
> — They may not remember the correct forms in the future.
> — Expect only as much as their current language level will allow.
> — Take care not to over-correct (which might worry them and make them lose confidence).
> — Don't stifle their creativity (which takes the fun out of a project).

When children are performing or showing their work, stand back – this is their time. Do not correct at this stage. It could discourage a child and damage their self-esteem.

When the project is finished, use it as an opportunity to praise and encourage the children.

LANGUAGE FOCUS 9.5

Useful expressions for correcting and improving children's language

1 Here are five corrections. There is one of pronunciation and one of writing. What kinds of errors are the other three teachers correcting?

a TEACHER: Let me just check.
      Let's see. These are fine.
      But here – what's
      missing? *u, v, w, x, z*?
   CHILD : *y*.
   TEACHER: Yes – *y*, good.

b TEACHER: That's a really good
      word, but can you check the
      spelling? What do you think it
      should be? Look it up!

c CHILD : Gloves.
   TEACHER: Are they gloves or
      mittens? Look – no fingers!
   CHILD : Mittens.
   TEACHER : Mittens, right.

d TEACHER: Listen carefully! I didn't
      say 'How many calendars?'
      but 'Where's the calendar?'

e TEACHER: No, not 'He's music' –
      He's …? Yes? – He's listening
      to music.

f CHILD: Spier.
   TEACHER: Can you repeat that,
      please – spider.
   CHILD: (very quietly) Spider.
   TEACHER: (nodding) One more
      time? A bit louder?
   CHILD: Spider.
   TEACHER: Good!

RECORD 2 Read these examples again, out loud, then record yourself taking the teacher's part. Play it back – do you sound sufficiently encouraging?

Further ideas

↻ 1 Try out the Alva story or the story you made up in one of your classes. Prepare pictures for it, and prepare to tell it once and then retell it a second time in a different way.

RECORD Record the lesson where you do this.

Try to get the children's feedback. Did they like the story? Which bit did they like/not like? Can they think of a different/better ending? If they tell you this partly in their mother tongue, recast what they say in English as far as you can.

After the lesson, play back the tape and see what you notice about the way you told the story and the way the children reacted. Write notes on how you might do it next time.

2 Discuss project plans with another teacher if you can. Make any changes you feel necessary to the suggested schedule. Then try it out with one of your classes.

Keep a diary while you do this – fill it in after every lesson where you do something on the project.

Try to evaluate the project.

— What was the audience feed-back?
— Did the children enjoy preparing for it?
— Did they enjoy the final performance or display event?
— Would they like to do another different project next term?
— Have you noticed any differences in individual children? Are they more or less confident/talkative/willing to use English in class?

3 Read Chapter 2 from **Wright, Andrew. 1995.** *Storytelling with Children.* Oxford: Oxford University Press.

4 If you have a computer, take a look at these two Websites for storytelling/books for children.

http://www.storyarts.org/classroom/index.html

http://www.realbooks.co.uk/

10

Planning for effective use of English in the classroom

This unit looks at

- how you can help children **acquire** English through your own **effective** use of English
- how your coursebook is one resource among many other resources
- how detailed lesson preparation will help your own use of English in the classroom.

Introduction

As we said in the first unit, we all start learning our first language by listening and absorbing the sounds around us.

— Children can acquire a second language the same way. The more English they hear, the more they learn.
— Our natural linguistic processes help us to adapt and acquire language as we mature.

A new language in school is

— different from the other subjects children learn
— not just about learning facts and concepts
— about communicating, i.e. being able to understand and use the language to do things.

Teaching a new language to primary children is challenging for all teachers.

If you have the same mother tongue as your pupils, you

— have to maintain your own proficiency in English
— have the responsibility of using English with your children.

But you have several advantages. You

— come from the same society as your pupils
— know in what ways their first language can help them learn English.

> **REMEMBER**
> When you use English you are
> — showing children that this new language is another form of expression
> — showing them that it can be used to communicate like their own language and that it can be fun
> — opening doors to other cultures and customs
> — passing on your own attitude and beliefs about the different people who use this new language.

10.1 Helping children learn and improve

Throughout the book we have been looking at how you can use more English when you are teaching.

We have seen how you can use English to

— begin your class
— end your class
— talk about what you are doing during your class
— organize the children and tell them what to do
— tell them how to do things
— help and encourage your pupils by commenting on their work
— play games, sing songs, tell stories
— introduce new topics
— explain what you think
— praise and encourage your pupils
— talk to them about their personal lives.

REMEMBER

You can help your pupils understand what you say in English

with your	by using	and by
— tone of voice	— **gestures**	— using familiar contexts and topics
— eye contact	— facial expressions	— **rephrasing** what you say in as many ways as you can
	— pictures/diagrams	— occasional use of their mother tongue
	— real things	

Using the mother tongue

Generally in teaching, we move from what is known to what is new. So on the very first day when you start to teach English you can explain to children in their mother tongue how you are going to use English during English lessons.

Teachers have different approaches to how much mother tongue they use in their lessons:

— Some teachers try not to use mother tongue right from the start. They only use English even when they teach real beginners. Of course they allow their pupils to speak in their mother tongue. But the teacher **recasts** what the children say in English.
— Other teachers use mainly English and just give a word or explanation in mother tongue if some children really need to hear this or feel uneasy.
— If the teachers are good communicators, the children quickly get used to hearing only English and gradually learn to understand more and more.
— Some children may be slow to produce English themselves but listening to the teacher speaking English works in the end.

One of the most **effective** techniques is to respond to all your pupils' questions and comments in English.
In that way you are showing them
— that you are listening
— that you can do the same things in both languages
— how to say in English what they said in their own language
— that they should try and say more in English.

LANGUAGE FOCUS 10.1a

Responding to mother tongue talk

a Look at the following boxes. They contain a list of questions and comments from pupils in their mother tongue and the answers the teachers gave in English. We have translated the questions into English. The teachers' answers are mixed up.

☞ Match the questions and answers. The first one is done for you.

Children speaking in mother tongue	*Teacher repeating what children say in English*
CHILDREN: Teacher, can I … can I go home now?	TEACHER: Sorry?… you want to go home? – Yes, OK.
1 Can I do this with Marta?	a Yes, you have it … here … don't you remember?
2 I said that, too.	b What does *cooking* mean? OK … it's …
3 Look at mine, teacher.	
4 Can I go to the toilet now, please?	c Yes, you can do it together, but you have to be quiet.
5 Teacher – teacher –.	d Well, I didn't hear you. Say it in a loud voice!
6 Look – a bird – a bird.	
7 I think he's going to be *recognized* … isn't he?	e I don't know … let's see what happens …
8 I haven't got any card with red sweater written on it.	f OK, Ann, I'll look at it later.
	g Yes, but in English – not in Spanish!
9 What's *cooking*?	h OK, go to the toilet, but that's the last one today!
10 Can I tell you my answer?	i What do you want, David?
	j Yes, there's a bird.

b **Recasting**
In the first example, the teacher **recasts** (repeats what children say in their mother tongue in English) what the pupil was saying as well as answering.
    Recasting is a very important step in children's language development.
It helps
— children to know they are understood
— children's acquisition of English because they hear what they said repeated in English
— to strengthen the idea that they can communicate in English as they do in their mother tongue.

You may
— have to develop the habit of recasting
— just start by recasting single words into English, then short phrases, and so on.

Here are four examples of recasting from the classes used in this book.

Notice
— that there is recasting of single words, of phrases, and of longer stretches of talk
— how the teachers do not interrupt the flow of any activity when they recast.

1 Children preparing to do some drawing
TEACHER: Right, you need your notebooks, your pencils, and what else?
(Child speaks in mother tongue. He feels he needs an eraser for mistakes.)
TEACHER: An eraser – yes an eraser in case you make mistakes – an eraser.

2 Very young learners preparing to do a matching game in front of the class
TEACHER: OK, in the envelope you have some pictures – now take them out, OK, and put them in a line …
(Child speaks in mother tongue about putting them on the floor.)
TEACHER: Yes – on the floor – empty it on the floor – OK, you should have four pictures now – put them in a line on the floor.

3 Children finishing a writing exercise
CHILD: Teacher – teacher – finished!
TEACHER: You're finished? That's impossible – did you do it here or at home?
(Child explains in mother tongue that he did the exercise here.)
TEACHER: Here in class – very good – very good.

4 Teacher reading the story of Elmer with her class
TEACHER: When Elmer rejoined all the elephants …
(Child speaks for a while about how all the grey elephants standing in lines look like an army.)
TEACHER: Yes – it looks like an army of elephants – doesn't it? – all grey elephants –.

c Rephrasing what children say

When children start to use English in class, you should encourage them. If they make mistakes, one of the best techniques you can use is **rephrasing**. Changing what the child said in English into better English without any negative comment is very supportive. When you do this:
— you show that what they said was not perfect but that it doesn't matter
— you show that what the child is communicating is valuable
— you encourage the child to continue speaking by showing that they communicated successfully
— you are helping children improve as they hear the better version of what they were trying to say
— you are rephrasing for one child but usually other children are listening too.

Rephrasing is similar to what mothers and carers do with very young children (see **1.1**). They
— repeat what the child says and often add to it
— show that they understood by rephrasing and answering
— do not make comments about the form of language the child used.

We've seen that good teachers prefer rephrasing to telling the child he or she is wrong. In the lessons we recorded for this book, there were very few examples of direct correction of children's English grammar.

d Correcting your pupils

We have already talked about correction in 9.5. You are more likely to use a direct correction of the form of language when your pupils are going to perform or **display** their work to a wider audience.

The reasons for this are obvious to children as well. They naturally want to do well. Good correction techniques should mean that
— you use correction as a learning tool so that it helps your pupils to **acquire** English
— when you correct language, it is clear that you are not changing what a child is trying to say
— you are trying to help your pupils to make their meaning clearer.

Think about how you can do this when you are correcting speaking. It is helpful to distinguish between
— errors of form
— errors affecting meaning and comprehension.

LANGUAGE FOCUS 10.1b

When and how to correct

In the two lesson extracts below and on the next page, the teacher, Flaviana, is getting her class to retell the story of Croc's party (see page 87).

Extract 1

⟳ Cover up the right-hand column (Commentary) with a piece of plain paper (on which you can write you own responses). Read the Interaction column first and find four errors. Write down why you think the teacher handles each one as she does.

When you have written your ideas, uncover the right-hand column and compare responses. The commentary explains why she chooses to correct (or not to correct). Would you have done anything differently?

	Interaction	Commentary
Teacher	Yes – it was a beautiful party. OK, now, who wants to tell the whole story?	(This was the end of the first retelling.)
Vanessa	I!	Should be *Me* or *Can I?* or *Please!* Teacher ignores it, as the meaning and intention are both clear.
Teacher	OK, Vanessa, you start.	
Vanessa	Croc is sad, Croc is young. Croc is corocodil …	Pronunciation error. Teacher corrects by putting emphasis on **Croc**odile, as this word occurs many times in this story.
Teacher	**Croc**odile!	
Vanessa	I have got …	Error affecting meaning, so teacher corrects.
Teacher	He has got …	
Vanessa	He has got a big mouth, big teeth, and sad.	Error of form – verb is omitted. Teacher rephrases to correct, and then picks up Vanessa's idea to extend it.
Teacher	He is sad, yes. Why is he sad?	

Extract 2

Later the teacher, Flaviana, asks Giacomo to take over.

They complete the **Background** to the story, describing Al the alligator, then continue with the actual story. This extract also shows how a teacher can highlight the structure of a simple story: **Background** (setting and characters) – **Problem** – **Solution** (and how this happens) , page 115 – and at the end an **Evaluation** (as in Boxes 3 and 4 in 9.2, page 113).

↻   Again – cover up the right-hand column and read the Interaction column. Here there are several places where Giacomo does not understand, and three where he says the wrong words. Can you find them? What do you think Giacomo misunderstood in each case? How would you correct him?

	Interaction	Commentary
Teacher	Giacomo?	
Giacomo	He's green and brown … He's green and brown … young …	Wrong meaning. Teacher looks at other children to see if they agree or not.
Teacher	He's younger??	
Giacomo	… old!	
Children	… old!	
Teacher	He's seven, isn't he? Croc is young; he's two. So what is the problem in the story? What's the problem?	Teacher shows she agrees with the class response and gives the exact ages. Teacher highlights the shift to the next part of the story – the **problem**.
Child	The problem is corocodile	Pronunciation error. Teacher corrects by putting emphasis on **Croc**odile, as this word will occur many times in this story.
Teacher	**Croc**odile.	
Child	Crocodile is sad because … ugly.	Error of form – *he* is omitted. Teacher rephrases to correct. She then moves on to the **solution** part of the story.
Teacher	Because he's ugly, OK. OK, and who helps Croc? Who solves the problem? Who has an idea to solve the problem? Giacomo?	
Child	He's ugly.	Giacomo has not understood this and goes back to the earlier correction. Teacher repeats question.
Teacher	Who has an idea to solve the problem?	
Giacomo	… organize … a party	but Giacomo offers the solution, not understanding the meaning of *Who*.
Teacher	Who organizes a party?	Teacher tries another *Who* question, building on child's response.
Giacomo	uh uh	Giacomo may have misheard – hearing *he* instead of *who*, so he agrees.
Teacher	**Who** organizes a party?	Teacher stresses *Who* and finally Giacomo gets it right.
Giacomo	Al.	
Teacher	Al, very good. Al organizes a party.	Teacher rephrases, combining his last two responses.

Think about all the ways you can handle errors when children are speaking.
What do you normally do and why? Make your own list. Whatever way you choose to correct
— children should not be made to feel silly or bad
— children should always know that you are helping them. If you correct by looking – questioningly – at the whole class, the child who has spoken must not feel that he/she has done something bad
— praise every effort
— you should try to increase children's confidence and feeling of success. Every child who uses a new language shows a willingness to learn. This is wonderful. You want to encourage your pupils so always try to show your approval for their contributions: ... *really good, yes, good, much better, well done* ... .

And finish activities and lessons on a positive note: ... *that was well done – fantastic work – that was great – we'll continue tomorrow.*

10.2 Using your coursebook as a resource

Many of the lessons we looked at and listened to in this book were connected with the coursebook the teacher was using.
In some of the lessons the teacher was
— using the coursebook
— extending a topic from the coursebook with her own materials and activities
— using the accompanying workbook/resource book to do some extra activities
— adapting the coursebook activities.
So the coursebook supported the teachers in their lessons and helped them in their planning.

Most of these teachers were also following a planned programme set out by their Education Boards or the National Ministry of Education in their countries. Your own teaching programme will also be guided by such factors as
— age of your pupils
— level/levels you are teaching
— needs of the class you are teaching
— schemes of work in overall school plan
— wishes and hopes of parents and school authorities
— time allowed for language lessons in your school's timetable
— time allowed for teachers to prepare materials.

Coursebooks
— offer you a prepared set of classroom activities and language, so save time
— offer children a learning aid
— set general standards
— are colourful and attractive to children.

But the coursebook is not necessarily the teaching programme. It is one of the language resources you can use. Other important resources are:
— YOU yourself and the way you use English, the stories you tell, etc.
— story books
— picture and word cards for various uses
— a puppet
— wall displays
— masks
— posters
— real things
— photocopiable material
— cassettes
— video recorders
— computers.
This is a list of possible resources. They may or may not be available to you.

Your coursebook may be a main resource. Some of the things listed can be supplied by the publisher as a 'resource pack' for the coursebook. But many of these resources can be made and used by the children and then used again the following year. Using real things or home-made resources helps you to use a more active approach.

And active learning, as we have seen, is more real and more fun for children.

Here are some examples where teachers are basing their lessons on coursebooks.

a   **Using a coursebook topic**

When a topic, such as telling the time, comes up in a coursebook, it is always a good idea to
— make it an active learning experience
— expand by doing more activities to help children learn and understand
— make it more personal.

🎧 To practise both telling the time and counting, the teacher in **10A**, Juan, is playing a version of the game *What's the time Mr. Wolf?*

10 A

Game 'What's the time?'

(*Bell rings*.)

TEACHER: Oh the bell, the bell. Always the bell. Now we're going to play a game. The game's called 'Grandma what time is it?'
(*The children like this game and love playing it*.)

TEACHER: OK? OK, we'll make a line here. OK, children listen. OK, I'll be your Grandma and you have to ask me …

TEACHER AND CHILDREN TOGETHER: What time is it?

TEACHER: OK, good. So, you three, come on, pay attention. OK. Now everyone … OK.

CHILDREN: What time is it?

TEACHER: It's four o'clock.

TEACHER AND CHILDREN COUNT: One, two, three, four …

CHILDREN: What time is it?

TEACHER: It's three o'clock. One, two, three.
(*after the game, later in the class*)

TEACHER: OK, OK, Marta was eaten by the wolf. OK. Now Kevin … OK. OK, calm down. Noise! Noise!
    OK, OK, Kevin … Come here Kevin. You are the Grandma. And OK, eeeny meeny miny mo, OK, you can say the numbers and come on … Quiet everybody. Now pay attention, Kevin is going to say the numbers.

CHILDREN: What time is it?

TEACHER AND KEVIN: It's five o' clock.

CHILDREN: One, two, three, four, five …

Juan with seven to eight year olds.

In this situation, the children are actively learning how to count and how to tell the time in English. Active learning allows children to learn in the most natural way, by doing things. This association of language and action is a powerful memory aid.

LANGUAGE FOCUS 10.2a

Revision of classroom language functions

⚬ In **10A**, find and underline examples of Juan doing each of the following in English.
a Organizing the children and asking them to move
b Saying what is going to happen
c Using game language for equality and turn-giving
d Making comments on what is happening at the time
e Getting children to pay attention
Look again at what you underlined. Notice how much language the teacher used.

🎧 Listen to the phrases again on your CD and practise pronouncing them with suitable intonation.

RECORD Record them on to your cassette.

---

b **Using text-based activities**

> REMEMBER
> Listening and speaking are the first forms of communication in all languages. Reading and writing are the second skills children learn.

When children are used to listening and speaking in English, a well-illustrated coursebook is a useful support. When children can read and write, the coursebook becomes another source of **language input** which they can learn from on their own and gain great benefit from.

A matching activity

Now listen to Emi, the teacher in **10B**, getting her class to do an activity from their workbook.

Here the children are looking at pictures and reading descriptions. They have to read and match each description with the correct picture.

In **10B**, notice how much language the teacher is using with the children when giving instructions and telling them what to do. Because the lessons are all in English, children are getting good experience of English in use.

In this extract, the teacher uses a variety of basic grammar patterns – giving opportunities for the children to absorb them naturally and understand how they are used.

10B

Read and match

TEACHER: OK, we're going to do an activity from your class book. So page 43. Find the page and have you got your pencils?
(*A child asks the teacher something in the mother tongue.*)
TEACHER: Sorry? Yes, OK.
So now everyone you're going to work in pairs. And you have to look and find. Now look at your book. It's 11 o'clock and it's playtime in this school. Can you see the number? You have to find these people. There's a boy eating a sandwich yum yum yum. Can you see him in the picture? What number is it? Where is he?
CHILDREN: Oh … yes …
TEACHER: Can you see number ten? You have to look and find the people who are doing these things.
TEACHER: Now work in pairs. OK, Ann can you work with Helen. And you two work together. And you two and you three. And you sit down with Jane please. OK, do you understand? OK? Sure?
(*later in the class*)
TEACHER: OK, very good. Fantastic. So now can you tell me? You're going to read out the sentences and the others can call out the number. OK? You can start …
CHILD: Three boys are playing football.
CHILDREN: Number 4.

Emi with eleven to twelve year olds.

LANGUAGE FOCUS 10.2b

Useful phrases with common words and patterns

In **10B**, the aim of the lesson in the coursebooks is obviously practice of verbs in the present continuous form – *eating*, *playing*, etc. Let's look at the extra English the children hear from their teacher. For example, the teacher uses eight other verbs (*look*, *find*, *work*, *see*, *sit*, *read out*, *call out*, *tell me*).

1   Verb patterns. How many phrases can you find in **10B** containing each of these verbs? Practise saying the whole **phrase** they are used in:

     going to   have to   have got   can you   can

2   Find all the questions the teacher uses. There are around 12. How many different ways of asking questions does she use?

When you have found them, listen to them again on the CD and say them along with the teacher, using similar **intonation**.

3   Prepositions. Which two verbs are followed by *out*?
    Look up the word *out* in a learners' dictionary and see how many different meanings and uses it has. Choose three that might be useful for you and write them down in a longer sentence of your own.

Pronunciation point: silent letters

1   Which letters in the following words are not pronounced? Underline them.

     answer   knees   know   combing   wrong
     whoever   listen   write   lamb

2   Do you know any other common words in English with silent letters?

Before we go on to look at planning lessons, we hope that in this section on coursebooks you have noticed
— how the teachers used their coursebooks – extending the activities to increase their pupils' learning opportunities
— how much English they used while directing, organizing, talking about what was in the coursebook.

10.3 Planning your lessons

As primary teachers, you have to think about lon[...]
objectives and plan your scheme of work accordi[...]
how to use more English with your pupils.

As you prepare your various English courses, [...]
your planning into sections.

1 Before the course

Before you start a new term or a new class, think about how you can
— create a pleasant, relaxed atmosphere in your classroom
— arrange the room so that it is easy to move around
— make sure you have wall space for any displays you want to use and
  that there is space at the correct level, so that children can point out
  items in pictures
— if you do not stay in the same room, use fold-up cardboard displays,
  or roll-up friezes, or posters
— make displays that can be used and re-used for several language
  practice activities
— display children's work with their names
— let displays grow, but when children tire of them go on to
  something new
— start or increase your collection of nice activities for children who
  finish early or who are doing something separate, for example,
      small puzzles or picture-card games or a book to look at
— plan to connect some of the topics you use throughout the year, e.g.
      from pets at home to zoo animals.
Which of these do you already do? Tick (✔) those. Arrow (→) the ones
you have not done but would like to do in the future.

2 General lesson preparation

For any lesson it is always useful to
— remember that you teach English by using English in your lessons
— prepare all the materials you need beforehand
— think of your lessons as small steps and so sequence activities
  carefully. Try to have a quieter activity after a lively, energetic one.
  (In Juan's class, **9A**, a story follows a noisy game.)
— tell children what you are going to do and help them see the reasons
  for what they are doing
— have some clearly developed routines because children feel secure
  with patterns they can depend on
— remember what you know about how children acquire language
— ask yourself why you are doing each activity and what opportunities
  the children need to listen, speak, read, or write
— plan how you can make best use of the language the pupils are
  already familiar with
— plan good learning tasks for new language, where the **context** helps
  children to understand
— try to give individual attention to different children so they know you
  are **aware** of how they are getting on (you can do this with different
  children over a number of classes)
— decide how you want to group your pupils and where they need to be
  for the various activities you will use.

3 Specific language planning for a lesson

Prepare what you are going to say when you
— greet your pupils
— talk to your pupils as you start/finish your English lesson – different topics and routines
— set up an activity – arrange the room – organize your pupils – say what you are going to do – and give instructions
— speak to groups or pairs or individuals if you have the opportunity
— want to say something positive to your pupils.
There are many ways of organizing your lessons and you know your own situation best. Many teachers like to have a set plan that they follow to give a pattern to their lessons and help them plan efficiently. Always remember that you know your teaching situation best and you should develop your own plan to suit your classes and circumstances.

NOTE
There is no 'Further ideas' section in this unit, but please read 'Over to you' for lots of ideas on what to do next.

Over to you

In this book we have put forward our ideas on how you can help your primary school pupils acquire English.

If you have
— followed the units carefully and systematically
— recorded yourself regularly and listened to your recordings
— tried some things out in class
we hope
— that you have noticed an improvement in your use of English
— that you have enjoyed experiencing new ideas
— that you are motivated to continue.

Your work should certainly be more satisfying and rewarding, but it is not always easy to bring in new ideas and change the way you run your classroom. On courses that I (Mary) have run, we often ask the teachers to make suggestions and tell us what they think about their teaching. The following two comments are typical of the sorts of things they say.

'What I find most challenging is speaking to the children all the time in English. I have to try hard to do this and they are not used to it. The most satisfying thing is seeing them speak English – especially the beginners – they can only say simple phrases and isolated words but they like it.'
'Different pupils of different ages have very different needs. Working with younger children is fun – they always want to play, to sing, to do things like action rhymes. It can be very exhausting but it's a very rewarding job because children understand very quickly. They are able to store lots of new language – even structures – and their pronunciation is often very accurate.'

So it is not always easy, but do keep trying. Once children are familiar with the new activities, things will improve fast.

Some of the things teachers recommend for personal language development include:

1 Use a good learners' monolingual dictionary
   — to look up very common words, e.g. prepositions, or common nouns like *time, people, way, point;* read through the entries, practising any new phrases and patterns
   — to check a word (even if only to check a spelling): read the whole entry; you will find many common phrases and grammatical patterns associated with the word
   — to look up a new word: always look for the phrases and grammar patterns it is used with.
2 Write down two or three useful phrases each time you look up a word in a dictionary.
   — Practise these phrases to extend your own vocabulary and knowledge of typical phrases. Look out for similar ones while you are listening or reading.
3 Read something in English every day, no matter how short or how simple. Many teachers read children's books, as they are useful for phrases and grammatical patterns.
4 Read cartoon stories in English. They give lots of examples of colloquial spoken language in **context**.
5 Listen to an English-language programme on radio or television.
6 If you have access to a computer, find an email partner to write to in English and surf the Internet in English (we give some useful Websites in Resources, page 141).

In your classes
— Ask your children (in their mother tongue) what they like and don't like about learning English.
— Record one lesson a week/fortnight/month and listen to the recording. Reflect on what you learn from doing this.
— Record children in pairs or groups playing or singing in English. (The children in the classes recorded for this book were very proud to be recorded.)

— Make a checklist of things you want to try out in class and try them, recording the activity you do.
— Try keeping a journal of the things you try in lessons, and write down your reactions and suggestions in it.

In your school/area
— Suggest that your school/teachers' centre subscribes to an English teachers' magazine.
— Set up a local teachers' support group. Meet as often as possible. You may be able to share books and teaching ideas, or watch videos together in English.
— Exchange ideas and materials. Have contact arrangements set up, e.g. phone or email, so that you can help one another when needed.
— Suggest that different teachers attend conferences, local teachers' meetings, etc., and report back to the larger group.
— Start a newsletter with ideas and suggestions for teachers, supplied by teachers.

Now it really is 'over to you'. You have to be willing to try and to go on
— experimenting on how you can use more and more English in class
— planning for your own language improvement.

Finally, we would be very grateful if you would write to us (via the publisher) and tell us how you have used this book and give us your feedback.
   We wish you the very best in your future development!

Mary Slattery and Jane Willis
c/o Professional Publishing Department
ELT Division
Oxford University Press
Great Clarendon Street
Oxford
OX2 6DP
UK

Key to units

1.1 First language – second language, page 10

a The mother says around 12 phrases. The child says the same word 3 times.

LANGUAGE FOCUS 1.1, page 11

b 1 chocolate, chocolate ice-cream? No. It's not chocolate ice-cream …
2 Where are your shoes? Yes. Your shoes. Where are they?
3 T: Chocolate eggs. OK.
4 Yes, your shoes … Where are they?

PRONUNCIATION POINT, page 12

1 The dropped syllables are crossed out: *chocolate, every, different, favourite, comfortable, vegetable.*
You say two syllables in *chocolate, every, different,* and *favourite* and three in *comfortable* and *vegetable.*
2 All are pronounced /tʃ/ except *shoulders* which has /ʃ/.

1.3 Organizing your classroom, page 15

a Words to be underlined:
1F four; Move; back; without; noise; leave; five; any; more; left; ready; listen; listen; don't move; desks
1G now; put; away; going; else; going; quietly
1H finished; finished; What; want; Yes; no; else; Wait; break

LANGUAGE FOCUS 1.3, page 15

b Jane repeats and Cristina and Emi rephrase.
c The five pairs of opposites are: 1 and 5; 2 and 7; 3 and 9; 4 and 8; 6 and 10.

LANGUAGE FOCUS 1.4, page 17

a Phrases with similar meanings: 1 and 7, 2 and 4, 3 and 5, 8, and 9; 6 has no pair.
b Words or phrases you could change:
2 today, this afternoon, this lesson
3 for lunch, to play, for your next lesson
4 your drawings, your writing, the story
5 once more, twice more, two more times
6 on the shelves, back in the box
7 Wednesday, Thursday
8 Ana first, all behind John, behind the leader
9 going home time, lunch time, play-time.
c Anyone else? Someone else might like a go. Who else would like a go? What else could we write? Where else might it be?
d These words always come when the teacher starts to say something, to get the children to pay attention.

LANGUAGE FOCUS 1.5, page 18

a I'm going to talk to you about a new person; Let's take out a bit more; I'm going to show you his face; Now before I take him out
b Can anyone tell me who this is? Who do you think it is?

PRONUNCIATION POINT, page 23

2 c pronounced /s/ *pencil, face, dice, ceiling, bouncy*
c pronounced /k/ *fantastic, carrying, carefully, combing, physical*
c pronounced /ʃ/ *special, ocean*
You can hear some of these sounds in **2A, 2B, 2F, 2H,** and **2I**

2.3 Listening and doing – TPR, page 25

a
2 G
Rearranging the class

TEACHER: OK/I'll **show** you/but **first** of all/what do we **do**/when we're **learn**ing a **new song**?
Right/Everyone come out **here**/to the **front** of the **class**/Uh uh
Now/let's **start** with the **first** row/**You** go over **there**/and **leave** a **space**/Now the **next** row./And **now** this one./OK

LANGUAGE FOCUS 2.4, page 28

a 1, 8, 9, 4, 6, 7, 2, 10, 11, 12, 3, 5

Unit 3   pages 32 – 41

3.1   Listen and colour, page 33

a   a picture for (2); give it to (2); his nose (2); colour the nose black (2)

b   a picture for Lucy – give it to Lucy; point to the nose – where is his nose; show me the eyes, the clown's eyes; show me … point to

c   point to the nose – where's his nose – yes, there it is show me the eyes, the clown's eyes – yes, here they are let's check now – show me … point to … black nose, blue eyes, orange mouth, etc.

d   colour the nose black; colour the eyes blue

e   Very good, that's really nice, good; great. Very good (2); Very good, they are lovely

f   Everyone has to colour their own picture. Please sit down Andy. Thanks

LANGUAGE FOCUS 3.2a, page 36

1   a   1f; 2g; 3d; 4b; 5c; 7a; 8e

b   6; h

LANGUAGE FOCUS 3.2b, page 37

2   Asking who wants a turn.
Some possible responses (there are many others):
— Who wants to start? Hands up! OK, you first, then you and then you …
— Whose go is it? Your go, Robert? Is it you next?
— Whose turn is it to do a mime? Your turn, Dominique?
— One more go. Who wants the last go? You do Lara? OK, quickly then.
— Blue team? But you started last time. So what about the pink team this time.
— Maria again? But you've just had a go. Who hasn't had a go at all? Enrico?

— Who has still not had a turn? A few of you over there at the back? One of you?
— Who still wants a go? No one else. OK.
— Which group has not been? Oh – sorry – your group, Leila! I missed you out …

LANGUAGE FOCUS 3.3a, page 39

a   The odd one out is 'One between two desks' because it is the only one which does not show pupils how to make the card. It is simply about giving out the scissors.

LANGUAGE FOCUS 3.3b, page 39

b   round (6); up (1); down (3); back (2); on (3)

PRONUNCIATION POINT, page 40

1   Unvoiced *th* sound /θ/ *thanks, three, throw, thin*
Voiced *th* sound /ð/ *this, that, there, the, they, mother*
Stick out your tongue between your teeth to help you say these sounds.
You can hear these sounds in **3A**, **3C**, and **3D**.

3.3   Topic Talk: Festivals and celebrations, page 41

Questions you might ask:
When is this festival? Does everybody celebrate it or just some people?
What do people do? Do you go to church, chapel, the temple, the mosque? somewhere else?
What do they wear? Anything special?
What do people eat? Anything special?
Do people give/get presents? Cards? Flowers?
Do you have a party? Where? What happens?
How do you and your family prepare for it?

You might also use these questions to help plan your talk.

Unit 4   pages 42 – 53

4.1   Using classroom phrases, page 43

1   Sorry, but I've forgotten my pencils
2   Please, Miss Bates, I can't see the board.
3   Sorry I'm late. I missed the bus.

LANGUAGE FOCUS 4.1, page 44

a   Some possible answers:

Child	Teacher
I've lost my colours.	Don't worry I've got a spare set here.
I've forgotten my book.	Did you leave it at home? OK, never mind.
I haven't got my pencils.	Who's got a spare pencil?

LANGUAGE FOCUS 4.2, page 46

From softest to loudest: 2, 1, 5, 4, 3

LANGUAGE FOCUS 4.3, page 49

a   *Wh-* questions: Which house does he go in?

b   A kangaroo? An elephant?

c   Is this a dog …?

d   And this is?

e   *Either/or* questions: Is this a mouse or a frog?

PRONUNCIATION POINT, page 49

1   /f/
Other common words with /f/ pronunciation are: *enough, rough, photo, phone, wolf, fine*.

2   /dʒ/
Other common words with /dʒ/ pronunciation are: *change, age, giant, jelly, juice, jet*.

4.5 Topic Talk: Animals, page 53

  a Here are some examples. Note that some animals might go in more than one list.
- Pets: cats, dogs, rabbits, guinea pigs, hamsters, gerbils, mice, fish
- Farm animals: goats, sheep, cows, pigs, horses, donkeys, chickens
- Wild/zoo animals: monkeys, zebras, lions, tigers, wolves, deer, elephants, kangaroos, pandas
- Nasty or scary animals: lions, snakes, hyenas, wolves, black bears

  b Things you might say about them:
- They live in/come from hot/cold countries; deserts/forests/hills/mountains.
- They live in small/large groups or herds.
- They like eating leaves/grass/seeds/insects/small animals/people!

Possible questions:
- What colour are they usually? What do they look like? What do they eat?
- Can they go fast? Are they dangerous to humans?

Unit 5 pages 54 – 65

LANGUAGE FOCUS 5.2, page 57

  a The correct order is: 2, 3, 1.

  b There are seven initiations and six follow-ups.
She rephrases in all six follow-ups, and extends in five (in the final one more than all the rest).

LANGUAGE FOCUS 5.3a, page 59

  b throw, catch, drop, pass, kick, bounce, roll, shoot/get a goal, lose, find, fetch, hide (also, players sign balls, you can break windows with balls).

  c Throw it away now.

PRONUNCIATION POINT, page 65

  1 When people are speaking **spontaneously** in English they link words together in phrases.

This is what the teacher was helping his pupils to do in **5E**. These phrases are said as if they are written together, e.g. *Tellusagain … Putitall*.

If you need to, listen again to the teacher saying these phrases. Notice how the last consonant sound is linked to the first vowel sound of the next word. And how sometimes a sound can disappear, e.g. *hands up* can sound like *hansup*.

In some phrases this link can sound like another sound, e.g. *would you like* in connected speech is /wʊdʒəlaɪk/

  2 *soccer, comic, want* have the sound /ɒ/
brother, mother, months have the sound /ʌ/

Unit 6 pages 66 – 81

LANGUAGE FOCUS 6.2, page 73

  a
- Who can **tell** me **this** one?
- **Anything** else?
- Or how about **this** one then?
- …you have to **guess** which **word** this is …
- **what** else?
- …you **come** out and **choose** one.

  b This one is not about guessing: *Let's put everything away.*

6.2 Topic Talk: Holidays/Vacations, page 76

Five possible questions:
- Who do people go with when they go on holiday?
- Where do people stay when they go on holiday?
- What would be a dream holiday for you and what would you need to really enjoy it?
- What kinds of holidays can people go on today?
- What do people do on holidays?

PRONUNCIATION POINT, page 79

  1 *walk* and *talk* have the sound /ɔ/. You don't pronounce the *l. word, work,* and *shirt* have the sound /ɜː/ in British English and you don't hear the *r* sound.

In some other accents you do hear a light *r* sound. Listen to the American speakers on the CD – do you hear the *r* sound?

  2 The word *sort* has the same vowel sound as *walk* /ɔː/. Some speakers lightly pronounce the *r* and some do not.

Unit 7 pages 82–95

LANGUAGE FOCUS 7.1a, page 83

Politeness phrases

a TEACHER: good – that's a good *c*.
CHILD: Thank you.

b TEACHER: Oh good *a* Midori. How are you?
CHILD (MIDORI): I'm fine.
TEACHER: Good.

LANGUAGE FOCUS 7.1b, page 84

1 **c** Don't just leave it **beside your chair**, where someone might fall over it.

2 The stressed words are underlined:
— the <u>orange</u> team
— now, <u>one</u> person at a time
— the <u>next</u> one writes *b* (maybe two stresses here)
— you have to do the <u>whole</u> thing
— all the way to <u>z</u>
— let's use <u>crayons</u>

PRONUNCIATION POINT, page 85

1 They are all the sound /ə/ which is called *schwa*. It is a vowel sound and it is pronounced but it is never found in **stressed** syllables. When native speakers are speaking naturally and at normal speed, this is the sound you hear in unstressed words, e.g. *a, at, from, the*.

2 *Team, need, piece, see, eat* all have the vowel sound /iː/ and *sit* has the sound /ɪ/.

LANGUAGE FOCUS 7.2b, page 88

1 opposites: a and c, e and b
odd one out: d

LANGUAGE FOCUS 7.2c, page 88

2 C: c, d, f, g; T: a, b, c, e, f

Unit 8 pages 96–107

8.1 **Telling a new story**, page 97

Rehearse it in your head, then write it down.
Read the story several times out loud.
Find or make pictures to go with the story, or practise drawing pictures on the blackboard.
Notice what the pictures are about and see how far the story language matches what is happening in the pictures.
Write down all key words, key phrases, and any repeated language.
Make a short summary.
Practise telling the story using the summary and using the pictures.

8.2 LANGUAGE FOCUS 8.2a, page 102

1 What did Elmer say?
Sh … sh … sh He said?
What did Elmer say?
What colour are elephant berries?
What colour?
See Elmer.
See them – see them – see all the berries.
Notice, too, how the teacher rephrased *large bush*, adding *very big bush* before she read *large bush*.

8.2 **Talking about what is happening**, page 102

a TEACHER: Did they know it was Elmer? Do they know Elmer?
TEACHER: Did they see him?
TEACHER: And are they happy?

b TEACHER: Good morning, elephant.
CHILDREN: Good morning.
TEACHER: They are very quiet.
CHILDREN: Very very quiet.
TEACHER: … Good morning.
CHILDREN: Good morning.
TEACHER: All grey elephants.
CHILDREN: Purple … purple …

c TEACHER: Well nearly grey … they were all standing quietly … see them standing quietly … you know 'be quiet' …

d TEACHER: Yes it looks like an army of elephants, doesn't it? Yes, and not smiling.
ONE CHILD: Purple – purple.
TEACHER: Well nearly grey.

e TEACHER: And he was pleased that he wasn't recognized. They didn't recognize him. They didn't recognize him …
Are they smiling? Are they happy? Not happy.
TEACHER: They are very quiet …
TEACHER: And are they happy?
CHILDREN: No.
TEACHER: Not smiling. Not happy.

PRONUNCIATION POINT, page 103

passed, walked end in /t/
pleased, recognized, rejoined, smiled, covered end in /d/
decorated ends in /ɪd/

LANGUAGE FOCUS 8.4, page 106

The key words stressed most are in bold and italic. Other words in bold are stressed but not as much as these.

---

8 E

TEACHER: Now *this* story is called 'The **Real** Story of the Three Little **Pigs**'. And the **wolf** is telling the story. **What** do you **think** the **wolf** is going to **say**?

CHILD: …

TEACHER: **So** he's going to **say**, '**Yes** I'm very **bad**. I **ate** the three little pigs.' What **else** do you think he's going to say?

CHILD: …

TEACHER: So he's going to **say** 'I said **please op**en the **door** and **they said 'no'** they were **so** *rude*. They were **so** *rude*.' **OK** and … **Yes, Narn**?

NARN: …

TEACHER: So, '***I'm*** your mum.' That sounds like *Little Red Rid*ing Hood.

Unit 9   pages 108–19

PRONUNCIATION POINT, page 113

These two words start with /s/: *surprise, supermarket*
— *story, stamp, stand, step, start,* /st/
— *snap, sneeze* /sn/
— *slap, sleep* /sl/
— *strawberries* /str/

LANGUAGE FOCUS 9.5, pages 118–9

1 a Writing
   b Spelling
   c Wrong word (could be either speaking or writing)
   d Children have misunderstood/not heard the question word, and have answered the wrong question.
   e A speaking error: in describing the picture, the child has omitted the verb.
   f Pronunciation: the child did not say the middle consonant.

Unit 10   pages 120–32

LANGUAGE FOCUS 10.1a, page 122

a 1c, 2d, 3f, 4h, 5i, 6j, 7e, 8a, 9b, 10g

LANGUAGE FOCUS 10. 2a, page 129

a …OK we'll make a line here …
     OK children listen. OK, I'll be your Grandma and you have to ask me …
     Come here Kevin. You are the Grandma.
b Now we're going to play a game.…
     … Kevin is going to say the numbers.
c OK Kevin … Come here …
     … Kevin. You are the Grandma. And OK eeeny meeny miny mo, OK, you can say the numbers and …
d Oh the bell, the bell. Always the bell.
     Noise! Noise!
e OK children listen.
     So, you three, come on, pay attention.
     Now everyone … OK.
     OK, calm down.
     Quiet everybody.
     Now pay attention, …

LANGUAGE FOCUS 10. 2b, page 130

1 *going to*: 3; *have to*: 3; *can you*: 5; *have got*: 1.
2 Five different ways of asking questions:
     One word with rising intonation: *Sorry?Sure? OK?*
     Wh- questions: *What number is it? Where is he?*
     Changing word order, e.g. *Have you got …?*
     Can you questions, for checking, e.g. *Can you see him in the picture?*
     Do you question
3 *read out, call out*

PRONUNCIATION POINT, page 130

1 *answer, knees, know, combing, wrong, whoever, listen, write, lamb*
2 Other common words with silent letters are:
     half, who, whoever, whose, hour, climb, wrap, night, right, castle, Wednesday, talk, walk, honest, knock.

Contents of the CD

Resources

Recommended reading

Brewster, J., G. Ellis, and D. Girard 1992.
The Primary English Teacher's Guide. London, Penguin.
A very useful and comprehensive book.

Donaldson, M. 1978.
Children's Minds. London, Fontana.
Great insights into how children think and learn.

Ellis, G. and J. Brewster 1991.
The Storytelling Handbook for Primary Teachers. London, Penguin.
A useful book which links storytelling to other areas of the curriculum.

Garvie, E. 1989.
Story as Vehicle. Clevedon, Multilingual Matters.
A wide ranging book looking at how stories fit into language teaching.

Gika, A-S. and W. Superfine (eds.) 1998.
Young Learners: Creating a Positive and Practical Learning Environment. Papers from Joint Conference in Madrid. Whitstable, Kent, IATEFL.
Fourteen very interesting papers with theoretical discussions of issues and practical suggestions for the classroom.

Halliwell, S. 1992.
Teaching English in the Primary Classroom. Harlow, Longman.
Covers many aspects of teaching language, with practical suggestions.

Lightbrown, P. M. and N. Spada. 1999.
How Languages are Learned. 2nd edition. Oxford: Oxford University Press.

Moon, J. 2000.
Children Learning English. Oxford, Macmillan Heinemann.

Rosen, B. 1991.
Shapers and Polishers. Cheltenham, Mary Glasgow Publications.
A book to encourage teachers to become storytellers.

Scott, W. A. and L. H. Ytreberg 1990.
Teaching English to Children. Harlow, Longman.
A very useful book for teachers, with practical ideas and useful activities.

Willis, J. 1996.
A Framework for Task-Based Learning. Harlow, Longman.

Practical activities and resources

Asher, J. 1965.
Learning Another Language through Actions: The Complete Teacher's Guide. Los Gatos, CA, Sky Oaks Publications.
Total Physical Response activities.

Briggs, R. and G. Ellis 1995.
The Snowman. Oxford, Oxford University Press.
The original story with added text and activities for young learners of English.

Byrne, J. and A. Waugh 1982.
Jingle Bells and Other Songs. Oxford, Oxford University Press.

Corbett, P. and C. McLean.
The Kingfisher Playtime Treasury. London, Kingfisher Nursery Library.
Other titles in this series contain a useful selection of movement rhymes for very young learners.

Gardner, B. and F. Gardner 2000.
Classroom English (Oxford Basics). Oxford, Oxford University Press.
Simple expressions and phrases for use in the classroom.

Graham, Carolyn 1980.
Jazz Chants for Children. Oxford, Oxford University Press.

Gray, K. (ed.) 1996.
Jet Primary Teachers' Resource Books 1 and 2. London, Delta Publishing.
A compilation of many useful photocopiable activities.

Heggie, A. 1989.
Bright Ideas for Early Years Art and Craft. Leamington Spa, Scholastic Publications.
Practical ideas for teachers working with 3 to 6 year olds. One of a series of very useful books.

Kalbag, A. and Jonathan Sheikh-Miller 1999.
Homework on Your Computer. London, Usborne Publishing.
Clear and well presented. Provides useful computer language support for teachers.

Lewis, G. and G. Bedson 1999.
Games for Children. Oxford, Oxford University Press.
A collection of games for children aged 4–12.

Meredith, S. 1999.
Starting Computers. London, Usborne Publishing.
Very good guidelines for teachers working with young beginners. Clear and helpful.

Moore, C.J. 1990.
Let's Write English. Oxford, Heinemann.
A helpful book on handwriting with practical work on letter recognition.

Palim, J. and P. Power 1990.
Jamboree. London, Longman.
Activities and photocopiable worksheets.

Philips, Sarah 1993.
Young Learners. Oxford, Oxford University Press.
Ideas and advice for teaching children aged 6–12.

Philips, Sarah 1999.
Drama with Children. Oxford, Oxford University Press.
Practical ideas to develop children's creativity, self-confidence, and speaking.

Reilly, Vanessa and Sheila M. Ward 1997.
Very Young Learners. Oxford, Oxford University Press.
Contains advice and ideas for teaching children aged 3–6. Lots of activities.

Ross, Mandy and Neal Layton 2000.
Alphapets. Loughborough, Ladybird Phonics Series.

This is part of a series of books designed to help children see the link between letters and the sounds they most often represent.

Smith, L. 1991.
Bright Ideas Timesavers. Leamington Spa, Scholastic Publications.
Contains photocopiable material for busy teachers, ranging from badges to special occasions, with a very useful section on world festivals.

Whiteford, R. and **J. Fitzsimons** 1988.
Bright Ideas Display. Leamington Spa, Scholastic Publications.
Ideas and suggestions on display. These last two books are part of a series of very practical books for teachers, originally aimed at English-speaking children.

Wright, A. 1995.
Storytelling with Children. Oxford, Oxford University Press.

Wright, A. 1997.
Creating Stories with Children. Oxford, Oxford University Press.
Interesting and valuable collection of ideas on how to use stories when teaching English. Lots of practical suggestions and activities.

Wright, A. 2000.
Art and Crafts with Children. Oxford, Oxford University Press.
Many creative ideas, plus tips on materials (including how to make play-dough).

Useful Websites

http://www.oup.co.uk/elt Click on 'Teacher's Club' and then 'Primary' to find extra resources and tips.

http://www.startwrite.com/ A Website offering handwriting software that will help you make your own material.

http://www.inspiration.com/ A Website offering mindmap software.

http://www.storyarts.org/classroom/index.html A Website for storytelling.

http://www.enchantedlearning.com/Rhymes.html A Website with nursery rhymes especially aimed at reading, with pictures for each rhyme.

http://www.designwest.com/Johanna/MotherGoose/ A Website with well-known rhymes.

http://www.ks-connection.org/penpal/penpal.html and http://www.epals.com/ Two Websites for pen-pals/epals.

http://www.realbooks.co.uk A Website with ideas and recommendations for using story books.

Stories

The following stories have all been used by teachers who found them suitable for their classes. We include them only as examples. As children and classes differ greatly, it is important to get some idea of what a book is about before you buy it. Then you can judge if it will suit your class.

Very big books

The following books are available as very big books. For that reason, teachers have recommended them for larger groups.

Farmer Duck **Martin Waddell** and **Helen Oxenbury** 1996. Walker Books. ISBN 0-7445-4779-2.

Handa's Surprise **Eileen Browne** 1997. Walker. ISBN 0-7445-5473-X.

I Love Animals **Flora Mc Donnell** 1996. Walker. ISBN 0-7445- 43924.

Tidy Titch Author-Illustrator **Pat Hutchins** 1993. Red Fox. ISBN 0-09-920741-9.

Titch Author-Illustrator **Pat Hutchins** 1997. Red Fox. ISBN 0-09-926253-3.

We're Going on a Bear Hunt **Michael Rosen** and **Helen Oxenbury** 1996. Walker. ISBN 0-7445-4781-4.

Books for reading aloud

The following books have been recommended by teachers for reading aloud.

Alexander and the Terrible, Horrible, No Good, Very Bad Day **Judith Viorst** 1987. Reissue Atheneum. ISBN 0689711735.

Brown Bear, Brown Bear, What do you See? **Bill Martin** Jr. and **Eric Carle** 1995. Puffin. ISBN 0-14-050296-3.

Busy Year **Leo Lionni** 1992. A.A. Knopf. ISBN 0679824642.

Dear Zoo **Rod Campbell** 1987. Campbell Blackie. ISBN 1852920025.

Doctor De Sota **William Steig** 1990. Turtleback. ISBN 0606032282.

Dinosaur Roar **Paul** and **Henrietta Stickland** 2000. Puffin Books. ISBN 0140566961.

The Elephant and the Bad Baby **Elfrida Vipont** and **Raymond Briggs** 1971. Penguin. ISBN 0-14-050048-0.

Elmer: The Story of a Patchwork Elephant **David Mc Kee** 1990. Red Fox. ISBN 0-09-969720-3.

Elmer Again **David Mc Kee** 1993. Red Fox. ISBN 0-09-991720-3.

The Gigantic Turnip Author **A. Tolstoy**, Illustrator **Niamh Sharkey** 1999. Barefoot. ISBN 1-902283-29-5.

The Hedgehog's Balloon **Nick Butterworth** 1999. Picture Lions. ISBN 0006646956.

The Itsy Bitsy Spider **Iza Trapani** 1998. Whispering Coyote Press. ISBN 1879085771.

Ketchup on your Cornflakes **Nick Sharratt** 1996. Hippo. ISBN 0590136631.

Meg and Mog **Helen Nicoll** and **Jan Pienkowski** 1975. Puffin. ISBN 0-14-050117-7.

The Mixed-up Cameleon **Eric Carle** 1988. Penguin. ISBN 0-14 050642-X.

Polar Bear, Polar Bear, What do you Hear? **Bill Martin** Jr. and **Eric Carle** 1994. Penguin. ISBN 0-14-054519-0.

Rosie's Walk **Pat Hutchins** 1970. Penguin. ISBN 0-14-050032-4.

Rotten Ralph **Jack Gantos** 1988. Houghton Mifflin Co. ISBN 0395292026.

Small Brown Dog's Bad Remembering Day **Mike Gibbie** and **Barbara Nascimbeni** 2000. Macmillan. ISBN 0-333-74539-6.

Strega Nona **Tomie de Paola** 1988. Simon and Schuster. ISBN 0671666061.

Swimmy **Leo Lionni** 1991. Random House. ISBN 0394826205.

Ten-in-the-Bed **Penny Dale** 1998. Walker. ISBN 0-7445-1340-5.

Ten out of Bed **Penny Dale** 1996. Walker. ISBN 0-7445-4383-5.

The True Story of the Three Little Pigs **Jon Scieska** 1991. Penguin. 0-14-054056-3.

The Very Hungry Caterpillar **Eric Carle** 1974. Penguin. ISBN 0-14-050087-1.

This is the Bear **Sarah Hayes** and **Helen Craig** 1994. Walker. ISBN 0-7445-3621-9.

Where's Spot? **Eric Hill** 1983. Puffin. ISBN 0-14-050420-6.

About the teachers

Some of the teachers who recorded their classes for this book sent us some information about themselves. We have summarized what they wrote below.

JANE CADWALLADER has been teaching children in Spain for 20 years. She gives courses aimed at primary teachers for Local Education Authorities around the country and has written several coursebooks for children aged from six to eight.

CLARA ERMINI teaches pupils aged from eight to eleven in an elementary school in Rome. She has been working there for eleven years and her classes usually have between 23 and 25 pupils. Clara has also been working as a teacher trainer for the last five years. She uses flashcards, Cuisenaire rods, and stories all the time in her teaching and believes that Total Physical Response activities are very important with young learners as they help them feel more confident.

CRISTINA FERNÁNDEZ is teaching in a school in Buitrago del Lozoya, to the north of Madrid. She has been teaching English for five years, in different schools in Madrid. She likes teaching English very much.

PURA MARÍA GARCÍA has taught English at primary and secondary school since 1985 and also worked with Teacher Training Centres in Spain. She now works with the Primary Publishing Department of Oxford University Press in Spain.

BOB JONES has taught English in Japan to both children and adults since 1990. His first job was with a city board of education but he now teaches small groups of up to eight pupils in his own school. He uses commercial textbooks but also enjoys making his own materials. Whenever he visits a new Japanese town, he checks out the local '100 Yen' shop. You can get toys, games, plastic animals, etc. and everything is the same price – 100 yen, which is very cheap. Very useful in the classroom and very affordable.

JUAN MORALES teaches in Tenerife. He teaches English to children aged between five and nine and likes to have a very positive atmosphere in his classroom. He uses a lot of variety in his lessons, changing frequently between active and restful activities. Juan finds it very helpful to be part of a teachers' group. With María de Armas Cruz, Candelaria Castellano, and Soraya Montesino, Juan regularly works on materials development. All the group participants use these materials in their classes.

ERIN E. NELSON has been teaching primary English in Kanagawa, Japan, for one year. Before this she taught older children and adults. She works in a language school with pupils aged from two-and-a-half years to six years. She found that the use of a puppet for the first few weeks was very useful in making the kids comfortable. Erin also realized that she had to act really silly (funny faces, strange voices, and exaggerated actions) at times, but the kids loved this, of course. Being sensitive to them as people is something she always keeps in mind as an hour in another language can be a little scary for some of the kids.

SUSAN ÖZBEK, CANDACE PLEKEITIS, KATHERINE SPRY all work in a primary school in Izmir, Turkey. They use a lot of 'native-speaker' stories in their classes and often choose books written for English-speaking children who are up to two years younger than their classes. They always want the children to enjoy the stories and have the satisfaction of understanding. Their classes have class libraries and even the youngest children enjoy looking at the illustrations in the books even before they can understand the text. There is also a home reading scheme in their school, which allows the children to enjoy sharing stories with their parents.

EMILIA ARTILES RUANO (EMI) teaches in Gran Canaria. Emi has been teaching for 13 years. Her classes usually have between 17 and 25 pupils. She has worked with pupils from six to eleven. She says 'I teach English so if I speak in English my pupils will try to do the same. They do not need to understand every word I say as my expression and gestures will help them understand. If I am unsure of something in English, I ask a colleague or another English speaker.'

FLAVIANA SORTINO has been teaching English in Lucca, Italy for five years. She works with pupils aged from seven to eleven. Her classes usually have between 16 and 25 pupils. She thinks it is important to speak English most of the time in the classroom because children are exposed to real chunks of the language and understand that English is a means of real communication with each other. They need to know lots of short sentences such as 'Can I go to the toilet?' or 'Pass me the pen'. Flaviana says, 'I find that children seem to learn very quickly through the use of stories, nursery rhymes, and songs. Children are motivated by listening to stories and telling stories because they are interested and the teacher can easily introduce new vocabulary and new structures.'

FUMIKO YAMAZAKI has been teaching primary English in Kitakyushu, Japan, for 21 years. She works mainly in a private elementary school with pupils from seven to twelve and with up to 40 pupils in any class. She normally uses a lot of teacher-made worksheets (developed with her colleague, Ms Hiroko Murakami), cards with pictures/letters, wall charts, picture dictionaries, and coursebooks for primary English. She gives her lessons almost entirely in English and she thinks pairwork and group work help her students to use more English and to develop their fluency.

Glossary

A list of language terms used in this book. Some of these words have a general meaning as well as a language-teaching meaning. You should look up a good language learners' dictionary to check the general meaning. Special words used for language work are marked 'special term'.

Grammatical notation *n.* = noun, *v.* = verb, *a.* = adjective, *adv.* = adverb
Phonemic notation IPA symbols are used. The bracketed sound /(ɹ)/ represents the letter *r* where it is pronounced lightly in some accents and not in others.
Stressed syllables are <u>underlined</u>.

absorb /əbz<u>ɔː</u>(ɹ)b/ *v.* to learn a language without noticing

accurate /<u>æ</u>kjərət/ *a.* correct, without mistakes

achieve /ət<u>ʃiː</u>v/ *v.* to complete something after making an effort. **achievement** *n.*

acquire /ək<u>waɪ</u>ə(ɹ)/ *v.* to learn a language naturally by hearing it, reading it, and using it. **acquisition** /ækwɪ<u>zɪ</u>ʃən/*n.* (special term)

alternative /ɔːl<u>tɜː</u>(ɹ)nətɪv/ *n.* different, something that you can do/use instead of something else

appropriate /əp<u>rəʊ</u>priət / *a.* suitable or right for a particular situation, person, etc.

associate /əs<u>əʊ</u>ʃieɪt/ *v.* to make a connection between people or things in your mind. **association** /əsəʊsie<u>ɪ</u>ʃən/ *n.*
1 connecting one person or thing in your mind
2 joining or working with another person or group

aware /ə<u>weə</u>(ɹ)/ *a.* conscious of something, knowing or realizing something. **awareness** *n.* Language awareness is when you get to know, or develop knowledge of, a word or phrase or a meaning or pattern

brainstorm /<u>breɪ</u>nstɔː(ɹ)m/ *v.* and *n.* when everyone offers as many ideas as possible in a short time, group sharing of all ideas, vocabulary items, etc.

caretaker talk /<u>keə</u>(ɹ)teɪkə(ɹ) tɔːk/ *n.* the speech used by mothers, fathers, and other people as they look after and care for babies and very young children. Caretaker talk encourages the children to talk. It has also been called parentese (special term)

chant /tʃɑːnt/ *n.* a word or group of words that is repeated rhythmically (often several times). In language teaching a chant is often a simple repetitious rhyme.

checking question /<u>tʃe</u>kɪŋ <u>kwest</u>ʃən/ *n.* a question you ask to see if children understand/have understood

chunk /tʃʌŋk/ *n.* words in a text or in speech that belong together, e.g. 'as a matter of fact'

clarify /<u>klæ</u>rɪfaɪ/ *v.* to explain so that someone understands

classify /<u>klæ</u>sɪfaɪ/ *v.* to put something or someone into a group with other things, animals, or people of a similar type

cognitive /<u>kɒ</u>gnɪtɪv/ *a.* describes the processes of thinking, remembering, understanding, etc. that are used in learning

collage /<u>kɒ</u>lɑːʒ/ *n.* a picture made by sticking together different materials such as pieces of paper, photos, etc.

combination /kɒmbɪ<u>neɪ</u>ʃən/ *n.* the bringing together of different things

concept /<u>kɒn</u>sept/ *n.* the general idea of something or the meaning in someone's mind

consolidate /kən<u>sɒ</u>lɪdeɪt/ *v.* to make something stronger and easier to remember

context /<u>kɒn</u>tekst/ *n.* the ideas, situations, information that help us understand. In language learning this also refers to words in a sentence that help us understand a new word or phrase

contrastive stress /kən<u>trɑː</u>stɪv stres/ *v.* more emphasis on one word to show the difference between one word and another

co-operation /kəʊɒpə<u>reɪ</u>ʃən/ *n.* working together with someone else to achieve something, helping one another in class. **co-operate** /kəʊ<u>ɒ</u>pəreɪt/ *v.*

copy /<u>kɒ</u>pi/ *v.* to do the same thing as someone else, mirror. **copy** *n.*

cross-curricular /krɒskə<u>rɪ</u>kjələ/ *a.* linking two school subjects, e.g. English and Science

Cuisenaire rods /kwɪzəneə<u>r</u>ɒdz / *n.* special wooden or plastic sticks of different lengths used in teaching mathematics. The rods are also used in language classes (special term)

discipline /<u>dɪ</u>sɪplɪn/ *v.* and *n.* getting children to behave well

display /dɪ<u>spleɪ</u>/ *v.* to put something in a place where people will see it. e.g children's drawings, a collage, frieze, etc. Also *n.*: a display

effective /ɪfektɪv/ *a.* works well, gives the result you want. *adv.* **effectively**

e.g. /iː dʒiː/ for example (abbreviation)

elicit /ɪlɪsɪt/ *v.* to ask careful questions to get children to answer. In language learning you are finding out if the children can use language (special term)

exchange /ɪkstʃeɪndʒ/ *n.* a short conversation between pupil and teacher which often consists of a question, a response, and a follow-up comment (also has other meanings)

focus /fəʊkəs/ *v.* to direct all the children's attention towards something in particular

frieze /friːz/ *n.* a long piece of paper often put on classroom walls with pictures or words, e.g. an alphabet frieze has the alphabet written on it with helpful pictures (special term)

gesture /dʒestʃə(ɹ)/ *n.* a movement with part of the body, e.g. the hands, the head

gist /dʒɪst/ *n.* general meaning

handle /hændəl/ *v.* to deal with (has other meanings)

interaction /ɪntərækʃn/ *n.* a two-way communication between people by speaking, listening, gestures, questions, and answers, etc. (special term)

intonation /ɪntəneɪʃən/ *n.* the rise and fall of your voice while you are speaking

key words /kiːwɜː(ɹ)dz/ *n.* the most important words

label /leɪbəl/ *v.* to write information about something on a piece of paper. You can then see the information when you look at the thing, picture, etc. Also *n.*: **label**. A piece of paper next to something, with its name on

language input /læŋgwɪdʒ ɪnpʊt/ *n.* the language that someone hears spoken or sees written down

mime /maɪm/ *v.* to act silently, without speaking

mind map /maɪnd mæp/ *n.* a diagram that shows how you can organize your thoughts about a topic or plan

mirror /mɪrə(ɹ)/ *v.* to copy, do or say what someone else does or says (has other meanings)

non-verbal /nɒnvɜː(ɹ)bəl/ *a.* a way of communicating without using language, e.g. with gestures, actions, movement

odd one out /ɒd wʌn aʊt/ *n.* the one that is different from the others in a group

phrase /freɪz/ *n.* a short group of words people often say; it may be easy to remember, e.g. *It doesn't matter*

play-dough /pleɪdəʊ/ *n.* soft coloured clay used by children to make models

plasticine /plæstɪsiːn/ *n.* material very like play-dough and also used by children to make models

predict /prɪdɪkt/ *v.* to say what will happen next. prediction *n.*

presentation /prezənteɪʃən/ *n.* to give an oral presentation is to talk to an audience about a topic in order to tell them about it

prompt /prɒmpt/ *v.* to encourage someone to continue by helping them

recast /riːkɑːst/ *v.* in this book we use this term to mean to repeat in English what a child has said in their mother tongue

rephrase /riːfreɪz/ *v.* to repeat children's speech in a different way, e.g. in better English

revise /rɪvaɪz/ *v.* to go over something again in order to learn it more effectively

roughly /rʌflɪ/ *adv.* generally, approximately.

routine /ruːtiːn/ *n.* the usual order or way in which you do things

schedule /ʃedjuːl/ or /ʃkedjuːl/ *n.* a plan of things that will happen or work to be done

set /set/ *n.* a group of things that belong together

set expressions /set ɪkspreʃənz/ *n.* useful phrases that children remember as a whole, e.g. *I've finished.* They can use them over and over again for particular situations, e.g. greetings

small-scale /smɔːl skeɪl/ *a.* not very big

spontaneously /spɒnteɪnɪəsli/ *adv.* speaking or writing naturally and freely without planning and without being asked

stimulate /stɪmjʊleɪt/ *v.* to encourage, prompt, elicit

stress /stres/ *n.* emphasis. *v.* to put force or emphasis on a word when you say it. Stressed words or parts of words are more clearly heard

summarize /sʌməraɪz/ *v.* to give a short *version*, paying more attention to main points than to details

sustained /səsteɪnd/ *a.* continuous, without interruption, e.g. sustained talk involves saying more than just a few words or phrases

syllable /sɪləbəl/ *n.* a part of a word that has a single vowel sound. Some words have only one syllable but others have two, three, even four or five – e.g. *the* (1), *even* (2), *syllable* (3), *co-operation* (5)

trace /treɪs/ *n.* to draw over lines to make them clearer. In many children's writing books letters are written in broken lines that they join up by tracing over them. Also in schools children often trace by putting a piece of transparent paper over a picture or lines and drawing over this

version /vɜː(ɹ)ʃən/ *n.* something spoken or written that you have changed to suit what you want

volume /vɒljuːm/ *n.* how loud a sound is

yucky /jʌki/ *a.* unpleasant or disgusting (informal)

yummy /jʌmi/ *a.* pleasant or delicious tasting (informal)

Acknowledgements

Some of these definitions are taken or adapted from the *Oxford Wordpower Dictionary*.

Index